Human Population Dynamics

Human Population Dynamics

With Applications To The U.S. 1790-2000

Lloyd Hogan

ISBN-13: 9781544256832
ISBN-10: 1544256833

Dedication

Elsie Madeline Walke Hogan
1927-1990

And

Minnie Belle Clark-Hogan

And

The young men and their wives who created
The Hogan Family, with roots in
Montserrat, Barbados, Jamaica, Venezuela, and Belize.

In their youth, they sailed from Barbados in 1907 and 1909 on the U.S.S. Ancon, headed for Panama to help dig that famous waterway uniting the Atlantic and Pacific Oceans. At its completion, they stayed on to help maintain the Canal Zone.

In the following years, they caused the birth of twenty-three children who became the first-generation Panamanians.

Today their descendants number in the hundreds, residing in Panama, the United States and many other parts of the world.

Five generations of births now define this clan.

To the Hogan Family and all its members yet unborn, this work is dedicated in peace and love.

Reader's Certificate #18

This certifies that

SHALOS SMITH

____,

The Reader

Is hereby inducted into the Human Population Dynamics Gang of 2

You are therefore entitled to all the rights and privileges of a reader, who, in consort with the author, make the book a functional reality. The author writes; you read; these two opposite functionaries are the necessary ingredients that unite to form the synthesis called Human Population Dynamics.

Lloyd Hogan
Author

Table of Contents

Preface

This study was started quite a few years ago. At the beginning it pretty much followed the standard methods of population analysis. It considered only the surviving segment of the population as the population. After all, dead people cannot perform any conscious act. And since populations are composed of people, only those who can exercise a conscious will were relevant.

It wasn't too long before I concluded that the dead segment of the population must be significant. After all, it was always present in consort with the survivors. It was apparent that both exhausted a common number of births. Omitting one from the analysis seemed to be a waste.

However, the reaction took the position that deaths were a factor that contributed to the reduction of survivors. After all, in any given quantity of births, the more deaths, the less survivors; likewise, the more survivors, the less deaths. The arithmetic gave perfect credence to this idea.

It then occurred to me that an alternative view of the facts was possible. After all, death could be interpreted as the difficulty of survival. A population in which there was relatively large number of deaths should exhibit relatively great difficulty of survival

A potent conclusion from this interpretation was that societies with relatively high death rates also had relatively high birth rates; societies with relatively low death rates also had relatively low birth rates. This thinking was driven by the assumption that births had to respond to the number of deaths. Death was the independent variable. The more deaths, the more births had to be made to overcome the deaths. The less deaths, the less number of births to overcome the deaths. Births and deaths thus moved in the same direction, with death leading the way.

In any event, this assumption did not lead to any clearer understanding of population dynamics and had to be abandoned.

The study seemed to undergo periodic discards and restarts. The prevailing scholarship was leading to a dead end. Finally, I made a critical decision to abandon the world of population research and seek other solutions. I went the way of the loner, going it solo in complete isolation from what was being accomplished elsewhere. As a result, the reader will find no citations, no bibliography, that supports or criticizes the ideas of this study.

I tried to adopt a position that population formation had to be a simple proposition. However, like all significant phenomena in the real world, especially those involving humans, complexity seems to hold sway. The task at hand was to seek an underlying mechanism that describes the phenomena in such a way that a simple scenario is still compatible with the apparent complexity.

This work is the result of those lonely endeavors.

I have no citations to offer. However, I must acknowledge a few people who have planted seeds of enlightenment into my skull.

Theodore Schultz was a master of suggesting ideas that lit the bulb in one's mind. His classification of societies based on the degree of "food drain" is one of those seminal thoughts that has percolated in my head for decades. I learned much from him in my youthful years.

Simon Kuznets' 1979 population book of essays has been a bosom companion of mine for many years. I owe him.

Tjalling Koopmans was a teacher whom I admired as a consummate scientist. His teachings and writings gave me a sense of what a disciplined thinker is all about. I am grateful to him.

Robert S. Browne was a close friend for sixty-two years before his death in 2005. We became fellow graduate students, and were later close working colleagues at the Black Economic Research Center, which he founded in Harlem, N.Y. His imprint on my thinking is always present.

My daughter, Pauli Hogan, has been a patient listener and critic of every important phase in my thinking during the later years of the study's completion. She has my sincere thanks.

The work is designed for the layman and scholar alike. I especially hope that social scientists will read it with critical minds to ascertain if they can apply the methodology to their work. A way to handle the constraints on individual behavior is of moment. It doesn't ignore the apparent random behavior of individuals; it accommodates such behavior by locating it within the constraints that impose order and purpose to such activities.

I also hope that physical and biological scientists will read it with a critical eye. In the creation of the work many of the ideas of these scholars became more clearly understood by me.

Finally, I hope that this work will prove to be useful to everyone who reads it, and that it will open eyes to the significance of being an effective member of a population, a most important grouping of individual human beings which exemplifies the reproduction of the earth itself.

Durham, N.C.
April 2017

Introduction

> One day while helping a young woman and her three children across the street, her 5-year old son kept staring at me. Finally, he asked, with sympathetic concern for my plight: "Mister, how did you get old?"
>
> The profundity of this question astounded me. How could so young a lad think of such a meaningful question. In an attempt to come quickly to an answer I responded that I got old by trying to live a good life for the last eighty-seven years, and that I had some good luck along the way. In addition, I told him that about eighty years ago I was a young lad just like he is; and about eighty years from now he will be old like me.

Here on the side of the road a young lad and I were engaged in a discourse that forms the basis of this work. I am an image of his future; during the next eight decades he will grow to be old like me. I am also an image of his past; I am like his great grandfather of his ancestral beginning. He is an image of my past; it is from a lad like he many decades ago that I grew to be old. He is an image of my future; some of my great grandchildren are just as old as he.

For the last few decades I have been engaged in an intellectual struggle to develop an understanding of how populations originate, how they function and develop, how they finally come to end. In a very peculiar way, any population starts with the birth of babies. Any one of these babies comes forth into the world as a result of a binary operation between an adult male and an adult female. Each of these two adults was likewise issued into the world, sometime in the past, by the same binary operation between some other adult male and adult female. And sometime in the future, each of these babies will join with an adult opposite companion, to engage in the same type of binary operation, to create a future baby.

Here is the fundamental scenario—babies of the past survive to the present to become adults and to create more new babies; hence babies of the distant past ultimately cause babies of the distant future. The unity of past and future babies, intermediated by adult parents, constitutes what we shall come to postulate as the underlying process of population formation.

The development of a population member from a baby to an adult takes place over a period of time in which the life of such an individual must be preserved. She/he must daily consume some food to provide the vital energies that sustain a material basis of life. In addition, some housing, clothing, and other socially requisite materials must be consumed on a regular basis. At the same time, the food, clothing, and other social requisites must be produced by the exertion of human labor against the earth and must subsequently be distributed to any such individual.

Correspondingly, if any such individual is a population member at birth, then its parents, and the parents of its parents, and the parents of its parents' parents, must themselves be members of the same population. Furthermore, if we assume that the future offspring of such an individual will be a member of the same population, we now have a closed group of people, engaging in a social embrace among themselves, over a long historical period, reproducing themselves to the exclusion of all other groups of people.

The mechanism by such a group is able to survive as a cohesive social entity over the years, or centuries, or millennia is the appropriate problem for solution that should yield us an understanding human population dynamics.

How did you get old, is the seminal question posed by the five-year old. The rest of this work is designed to formulate a precise and unambiguous answer to this question.

At the atomic core of a population is the birth of individuals. These discrete units possess some interesting attributes, among which is life. As a matter of fact, the individual is life itself. This is a compound of nonphysical energy, encased in a material receptacle of inert energy. It has the ability to spontaneously act, to do things, to move. We call this ability a conscious will. The exercise of this will is the motive force for action.

At the atomic level of the population is the family. It is the arena into which the new born is ushered into the population, as a result of an operation involving two adult parents. The new born, and other children and adult member of the family, depend upon these parents for the maintenance of life.

The transit of the new born from birth into the cradle of its family maintenance operations, through a web of intricate social entanglements, to participate in population formation, is the stuff of which a population is made.

Before the new born starts its journey, one more essential condition is imposed on its behavior along the way. It is not the only birth taking place during the Current Year. It is only one among many born to other parents in the population that year. These births play a special role, indicated by the fact that their specific year of birth, the Current Year, the most recent year of formation of the population, is also the year of birth for the population as a whole.

This signal event is celebrated by encasing all the births of a given Current Year into a Quantum Cocoon. This keeps them forever united as one sub- atomic particle, composed of all births of the same year, giving it (and its constituent birth cohorts) a unique identity, while on the journey to population formation, and later as an integral part of the population membership.

The Quantum Cocoon's unique ID, consists of its specific year of birth and its age during the Current Year. We denote this ID by T(t,r), where T is the Current Year, t is the specific year of birth, and r is the age of the Quantum Cocoon during the Current Year.

For the duration of the transit through the interstices of population activities the ID enables us to keep track of the trail and location of the Cocoon. This is true for every Cocoon in the population. Every population member who was born prior to the Current Year also possesses its own specific ID.

The year of birth, t, component of the ID, stays with the Cocoon forever. The age, r, component changes by one year with the advent of a new set of annual births. This should not be mysterious. It marks the annual increment in the completion of life of the members of every Cocoon.

The trail of a Quantum Cocoon through the maze of population formation activities is what the social scientist refers to as the web of institutional constraints on individual behavior. We postulate the creation of a set of Gangs of 2, joined in a time-sequential pattern of motion that leads to the ultimate act of population formation.

The sequence encompasses the trail of the Quantum Cocoon from its origin in its own Gang of 2; its giving rise to the next Gang of 2; and so on, to the completion of the final task along the trail.

These Cocoons are aggregated over a relevant number of years to create a group of births, consisting of sub-groups which stand at the ready to create Human Labor.

Human Labor, in turn, reproduces not only the population membership, but also reproduces the food and other means of survival of population members.

Human Labor, being subject to the conscious decision of people, is executed under different rules of engagement. Each distinctive set of rules results in a distinctive Political Economy.

The Political Economy requires to be managed. This responsibility is accomplished by the Political State which promulgates, monitors, and enforces the rules of the Political Economy.

Finally, the Political State is impacted by all the Political States existing on the face of the earth. Not only these States, but the earth itself, is the geographic domain that provides all the human and non-human sources of the population and its means of survival.

This trail is the heart of the subject-matter of the study. We describe it in detail in three parts.

Part I consists of nine chapters, 1-9. It constructs a descriptive hypothesis of the origin, formation, growth, development, and final outcome of a human population. Eight chapters complete this phase of the work. We stress that everything in Part I is strictly hypothetical. The reader must not at any time consider it a true image of reality. It is only one, among an infinite number of possible simulations, of events of a real world phenomenon.

This is at the heart of our endeavors. Our purpose is to adhere to a principle in the pursuit of knowledge—construct an unambiguous and accurate description of the phenomenon under study before you can begin to explain it. The cardinal sin of many research studies is the rush to explanation without knowing what it is that is being explained.

The descriptive hypothesis is presented in the nine chapters. The hypothetical trail of a new birth through the many social constraints to its effective participation as a member of the population is the subject matter of these chapters. The objective here is to demonstrate that all the institutional constraints which are encountered by individuals in the quest for effective population membership seem to be complex beyond comprehension. Yet, all the obstacles are overcome by means of a principle of motion which we have labeled as the Gang of 2. This principle, aided by an ID system, makes the task quite simple.

Part 2 consists of four chapters, 10-13. The objective here is to interface the hypothetical population to real world populations. More particularly, we use the actual results from the population of the United States during the period 1790-2000 to disprove the hypothetical outcomes of our concocted population.

Unfortunately, not many crucial tests are possible. The main empirical test involves commanding the U.S. population to generate some Census results during the study period. We then generate the corresponding Active Population from our hypothesis and compare the two results.

Census data are presumably very well constructed real world descriptions. They are what our hypothesis refers to as Active Population, as distinct from Population, as the Census is referred to by practically everyone. Both mean the same thing—the surviving members of the population.

We caution the reader that our concept of a population consists of both survivors and deaths—survivors being Active Population and deaths being Inertial Births. Both of these subgroups of the population play a significant part in Human Labor. If we refer to the population as only the survivors, we have robbed ourselves of the knowledge of the true role of Human Labor as the crucial engine in the reproduction of both the population and its means of survival.

We should also be aware that our hypothetical Active Population carries marks of the deaths. In short, if we know the surviving segment of the population, we also know the dead segment. This suggests that the hypothetical population carries related information that may not be available in the archives of the real population.

Part 3 consists of three chapters, 14-16, which look to the future. We consider how the hypothesis may be used to analyze populations other than the U.S. We also discuss some insights from the study and make some speculations about the future.

As we mentioned in the Preface, this study was done in complete isolation from the existing body of work by population scholars. It will therefore bear the mark of apparent differences in concepts and differences in methods of approach. Nevertheless, it is hoped that population scholars will seriously try to digest this study and to merge it with their own. The objective is to enhance our understanding of how a human population originates, grows and develops, and how it comes to end.

Part I
A Hypothetical Description of a Human Population

1

Primer in Population Formation

A HUMAN POPULATION IS a highly specialized group of individual human beings. The specialization derives from the fact that the individuals are fused together in the performance of a continuing and stable set of activities which function to preserve the quantitative as well as the non-quantitative attributes of the group. It is a group of people that has been locked together in a social embrace, reproducing itself among itself to the exclusion of all other people, over a protracted period of time.

The exercise of conscious will, unique to each individual, is the motive force for action by the group. Yet, individual actions are at once subject to constraints imposed by the group upon itself. These constraints provide the distinguishing attributes of the group's genre.

Framework for Population Analysis

Popular conceptions that an individual act plays a major role in population formation must be abandoned. A special social framework of population analysis should help us understand how a population originates, functions, develops, and comes to end.

It is obvious that the motive force underlying population formation has to be the exercise of individual will. Active, living, purposeful individuals are the autonomous creators of activity in any social endeavor. We are dealing here, however, with a social organism, forged out of the actions of many individuals, over a protracted period of time, involving intricate interlacings of subgroups of individuals and events.

The conclusion to be drawn from all this is that the individual is absolutely necessary for population formation; however, its influence on the final outcome is practically nil. In what follows we present a framework which should lead to a better understanding of the mechanism of population formation.

We postulate the existence of six major conditions that frame population formation.

Individual Life Time
Aggregation of Births of Individuals
Human Labor Activity of Sub-groups of Births
Creation of a Political Economy
Political State Management of the Political Economy
World Environment of All Types of Political States

A single, discrete individual person, flushed with human energy, is the fundamental unit of a population. It is the seed that occupies the core of population reproductive activity.

Births of living individuals, arranged in strategic groups, stand at the ready to participate in specific aspects of population creation activities.

Human Labor, performed by groups of births, is the decisive predicate of population formation. It is the singular creative act that molds groups of births into a viable population engine.

The population so created is an integral component of a Political Economy, whose function is to simultaneously reproduce the population and its means of survival.

The rules which define the Political Economy as a specialized type of human labor are promulgated, monitored, and enforced by a Political State.

Finally, the Political State functions as one among all the various types of political states in the world. All these political states will have individual and combined impacts on the population formation in question.

Life Time of an Individual

Human life is the essential bundle of energy that drives all human activity and the results of such activity. It is the driving force for population formation. It must be understood that such life exists as a bundle of energy encased within the material form of the individual human being. Life is energy; human being is energy encased in a physical container called the human person. The start of a human population, therefore, must begin with the individual living human being.

The individual population member originates out of a birthing relationship, engaged in by two adult members of the population. The new population member is the result of this birthing operation. The new member comes to fruition within a family unit, consisting of the parents, other siblings, and other members. It goes without saying that all existing family members also originated from a birthing process prior to that of the new-born.

The new-born will depend upon the family for support until it reaches the age of adulthood. Among other things it will be subject to the capabilities of the family to provide it with food, housing, clothing, schooling, transportation, communication, and a host of other necessities for maintaining its life.

As a living human being, the new-born will engage in activities appropriate for its age and abilities to personally enjoy its tenure of existence. Simultaneously, it will age as the years go by. Its individual life is limited to a range of years of age between zero and 99 years.

The new-born comes into being as one member of a cocoon of annual births. We refer to this cocoon as the new-born's Quantum Cocoon of all birth cohorts during the Current Year. Each of the birth cohorts is a member of its own family. Thus, the number of families involved in a quantum of births is equal to the number of cohorts in the quantum. The quantum plays a major constraining role on the activities of the new-born population member. This constraint is further compounded by the birth quantum of every member within every family directly associated with the birth of the individual population member.

Every quantum of birth is immediately paired with an annual interval of time. It is placed in a unique time-dependent slot. This is a necessary condition for creating strategic groups of population members who can be in a ready state to perform specialized population reproduction tasks.

The unique slot may be conceived as an ID. This ID consists of a pair of elements—specific year of birth, and age during the Current Year. The sum of these two elements is identically equal to the Current Year.

The specific year of birth is the start of life of each member of a given quantum of births; the corresponding age during the current year is the end of life to date of each member of such a quantum of birth. Thus, every unique quantum of births is linked to the same Current Year. The Quantum Cocoon is therefore a designation for one individual year of life. The Current Year, which is a proxy for the Life of an Individual, is also a synthesis of its two opposite ID elements.

The basic fact to be derived from these considerations is that the start of life of one population member is immediately linked with a good number of existing population members. It is a member of a Quantum Cocoon, consisting of many members.

This one life is already connected with all its birth cohorts. It is likewise immediately connected with all the families of its birth cohorts. It is further connected with all the families of all its sibling's birth cohorts. In sum, immediately upon birth, it is in position deeply involved with may groupings of population members. But its positioning among all these groups is quite simple to locate because of its unique birth quantum ID.

Aggregate Births of Individuals

One living human person is the smallest unit of population formation. Every live birth of such a person during a given year is a member of a quantum of births. Each member of the quantum is also a member of a family. It follows that one quantum of births resides in as many families as the number of members in the quantum.

Since the family is made up of population members, it follows that each of the family members are members of its unique quantum of births. So that each member's quantum of birth is shared among a number of families equal to the number of births in its quantum.

The population is poised to becoming a reality by the activity of aggregating quanta of births. These aggregates become special groups of births, standing at the ready to carry out strategic components of population formation activities. Aggregation is easily accomplished since the births are tightly encased in time capsules with unique ID's. The aggregation is accomplished by summing all quanta of births over their relevant years of birth and age during the current year. It is akin to summing the number of births over an ascending set of positive integers; and the reverse sum over a related set of descending positive integers.

The aggregate so computed is the total number of births over a specific period of years. It is composed of the sum of two elements. One is the sum of a specific quanta of years of birth. This sum is the total number of survivors in that group. The second is the sum of quanta of years of age during the current year. This sum is the total number of deaths for that group.

Aggregate births are a synthesis of two opposites--survivors and dead. These are the critical groups of births which play important roles in population reproduction. We will henceforth refer to the survivors as the Active Population; the dead ones will be referred to as Inertial Births. One is alive and is capable of being an instrument of initiating population reproducing activities. The other is inactive, but serves as the object into which population reproducing activities are directed.

Human Labor

Human Labor, like all aspects of population formation, is the synthesis of two opposite elements-- human earth matter and non-human earth matter. Simply put, the synthesis comes about as a consequence of the transformation of non-human earth matter into human earth matter, and the simultaneous transformation of human earth matter into non-human earth matter.

Human Labor is the overriding social activity that drives the formation and development of a population. It is executed in two phases—Internal Labor and External Labor. It is performed autonomously by two major groups of births—Active Population and Inertial Births.

To unite the two phases of Labor it makes use of two institutions--a Conduit from Internal Labor to External Labor, and a Conduit from External Labor to Internal Labor.

To complete the cycle of Labor and to restart it on a new round, it makes use of two institutions--Accumulation of Internal Labor, and Accumulation of External Labor.

Human Labor comes in different configurations, depending upon the nature of the institutions it employs and the specific rules that guide the operations of these institutions. This defines the Political Economy in Force.

Role of the Political Economy

The Political Economy is a special application of Human Labor in the creation of the population. But it is more; it also encompasses the creation of the non-human means of survival of the human population as well.

Different types of Political Economies are distinguished by the kind of property relations which bind members of the population together. The types of property may also differ. The rules governing the acquisition and ceding of private property may differ among various types of Political Economies. Finally, division of the population members into different classes, based on private property ownership makes for different Political Economies.

Once we admit of possible differences among Political Economies, the necessity for the management of any specific Political Economy becomes evident. This role is the responsibility of the Political State.

Political State as Manager of the Political Economy

The political state is the command center of population reproduction activity. It has final say concerning how the Political Economy performs its task.

Its main functions are to promulgate, monitor, and enforce the rules of operation of the Political Economy. To accomplish its task it must be the most powerful institution in the society in order to receive acquiescence to its commands. It may also serve as advocate and protector in a world of other competing political states.

World Environment of Political States

Finally, population reproduction must take place in the context of many other political states throughout the world. We subscribe to the assumption that political states develop in an evolutionary sequence through distinct phases. We refer to the period of any one stage in this evolutionary process as the historical era of population formation. Hence, the world environment should consist of individual political states of every historical era existing side by side in real time.

The landscape is awash with all manner of differences—large and small, predatory and peaceful, nationalistic and cooperative, single and multiple languages, single and multiple religions.

In short, the world environment is a complex panorama of political states inhabited by populations of a wide range of different characteristics. But they share a common earth space.

The geographical base comes to the task with two types of material—human and non-human. Population reproduction can be conceived to be a systematic transformation of human earth matter into non-human earth matter; and the corresponding transformation of non-human earth matter into human earth matter in continuing periodic cycles.

The individual population member goes about his day to day activities making choices that appear to him to be made according to his free will. But so long as he is a population member, these choices occur within the limits imposed by all the constraining conditions of individual population member activity which we have alluded to in this framework for population analysis.

The constraints are not so much restrictions on behavior; they represent order and purpose and social dimension of population reproduction. The population is in complete dependence upon the role of every one of its individual members. However, the potency of the individual to affect population outcomes is practically zero.

Population as a Reproduction Activity

The power and dominance of all the constraints on individual behavior is so overwhelming that it would appear to obscure the essential role of the very core of a population. The individual member originated as a result of a birth relationship between a pair of adult population members, within the arena of a family. It is the seed of every population.

Populations exist for hundreds of years. In the cases of India and China it has been said that they were in existence for more than 10,000 years. The fact that the individual member is restricted to a longevity between zero and 99 years sets a rather meager limit to the active role of such an individual.

Individual members are therefore limited to the production of new members. Over time, some of these members will die. Even if some serve as replacements for a dead member, there is no essential connection between a dead member and such a replacement within a given family. Any such connection will be possible under the condition of a stable social relationship between different and possibly obscure families. In short, reproduction implies social relationships far beyond the control of any individuals involved.

A process of reproduction is a set of activities which preserves the population as the same genre of its historical era for long periods of time. A systematic renewal of membership with new births is a necessary part of the process.

We postulate that any process of reproduction must satisfy certain principles. It must make the present cycle the sink of the past; at the same time it must make the present cycle the fount of the future. The natural ending of a cycle of activity must also entail the beginning of a new cycle of repetition of the activity.

This is a summary view of population formation. It should guide us along the way as we consider in more detail the trail of the individual in all this from birth origin to full-fledged member of a population.

2

Pivotal Role of Birthing

In this chapter we postulate the existence of some essential conditions which help to determine the origin of a population member. These are:

1. Two adult parents who are population members.
2 A birthing operation which binds the parents.
3. A new population member resulting from the birthing operation
4. A family within which birth takes place
5. A Quantum Cocoon into which the birth is embedded
6. A population time-frame in which the new member is assigned a specific reserved location.

These conditions are among the class of constraints which begins the trail that sends the new-born on the way to becoming an effective participant in population formation activities. Ensuing chapters will discuss other essential conditions which ends the trail.

Source of Population Membership

Birthing of babies constitutes one of the fundamental activities of human population dynamics. It is the elementary source of population membership. Every population member originates from the earth as a new born baby through the instrumentality of its parents. But such a baby is one member of the most recent annual birth group of the population, whose birth groups span all years from year 1 to the current year, the age of the population itself. When one considers that some populations have persisted for many centuries, the new-born babies must be an extremely small part of the total population membership.

Nevertheless, no matter how proportionately small, the new-borns are a very necessary condition for the continued existence of the population. During the Current Year, some population members will have died at ages ranging from zero to 99; the others will be alive. Some of the new borns may well serve as replacements for some initial living members or for some initial dead members. Some may even play the role of increments to the current population over and above the initial population.

Table 2.1

Illustration of a Quantum Cocoon's ID: T(t,r)
For Six Years of Birthing

					6,0
				5,0	5,1
			4,0	4,1	4,2
		3,0	3,1	3,2	3,3
	2,0	2,1	2,2	2,3	2,4
1,0	1,1	1,2	1,3	1,4	1,5

Notes:

1. Each cell is a Quantum Cocoon's ID: T(t,r).
2. First member, t, is year of birth. Second member, r, is age during Current Year.
3. Each column represents all ID's for a given Current Year.
4. Each row represents the canging age of a specific Cocoon with change in years.
5. Every Cocoon in the same column has the sum of its elements equal to the Current Year.

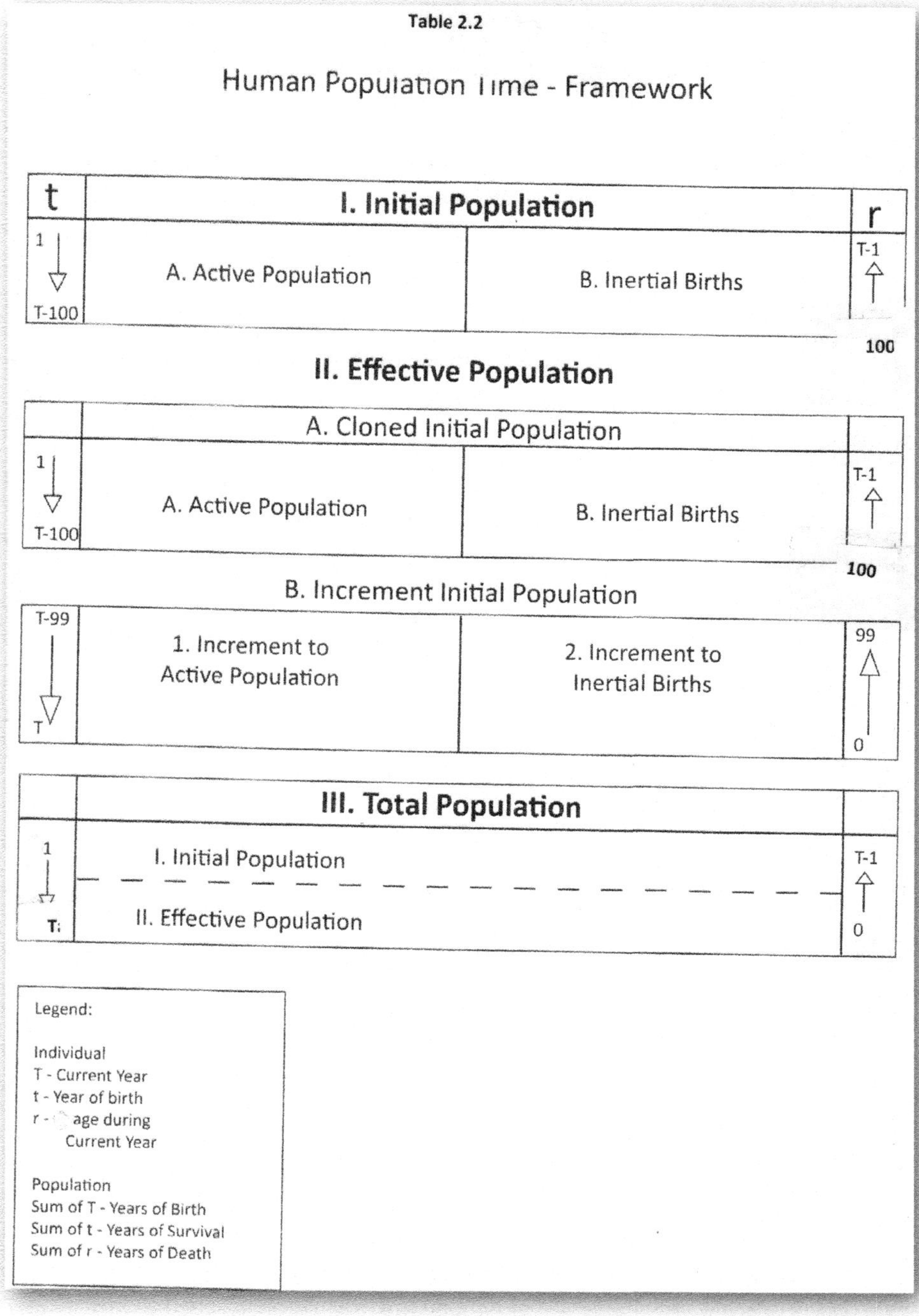
Table 2.2
Human Population Time - Framework
t
I. Initial Population
r
1
T-100
A. Active Population
B. Inertial Births
T-1
100
II. Effective Population
A. Cloned Initial Population
1
T-100
A. Active Population
B. Inertial Births
T-1
100
B. Increment Initial Population
T-99
T
1. Increment to
Active Population
2. Increment to
Inertial Births
99
0
III. Total Population
1
I. Initial Population
II. Effective Population
T-1
0
Legend:
Individual
T - Current Year
t - Year of birth
r - age during
Current Year
Population
Sum of T - Years of Birth
Sum of t - Years of Survival
Sum of r - Years of Death

The new-borns therefore have pervasive effects throughout the entire age structure of the population. They provide the essential material that refreshes the vital energies so necessary for the survival of the population over extended periods of time. So long as no untoward catastrophic event disrupts the unbroken annual sequence of births, the population is assured of a stream of new members as time goes on.

The population creation task is to arrange the set of individual births into a special cohesive social group.

Table 2.1 and Table 2.2 illustrate the temporal structure of births within a human population. To understand the dynamics of population formation this structure must be solidified in the mind to be used as an observational tool for recording population events in the real world.

Decoding the Population Time-Framework

These tables lend themselves to a very simple description of the birthing structure. The human population is made up of two major time-defined parts. One part is the Initial Population. This part consists of all births created during the Initial Period--the time span starting at year 1, and ending at year T-100. This period covers the entire span of years prior to the Current Cycle.

The second major part consists of all births created during the Current Cycle--the time period starting at year T-99 and ending at year T. The Current Cycle is assumed to be the most recent 100 years.

The Initial Population contains two segments. One segment is the Initial Active Population. This contains all births which were created during the Initial Cycle and which remained alive at the end of the initial period. It is therefore alive at the beginning of the Current Cycle.

The second segment is the Inertial Births. It contains all births which were created during the Initial period and which also died within that that period. They begin the Current Cycle in the dead state.

The second major part of the time frame is the Current Cycle. This Cycle takes place during the 100 year span from year (T-99) through year T. This span of years consists of two related sub-segments—(a) Replaced Initial Population and (b) Increment to the Initial Population.

The replaced Initial Population is divided into two sub-segments—Replaced Active Population and Replaced Inertial Births.

The Replaced Population is merely a "clone" of the Initial Population. It copies its quantitative magnitude. Since it is new births, it may well have changes in the non-quantitative traits of the members who make it up.

Increment to the Initial Population is likewise divided into two sub-segments—Increment to Active Population and Increment to Inertial Births.

We note at once that during the Current Cycle the Initial Active population will die, but will also be reproduced. It will also have the onus of producing all the births of the Current Cycle. The number of these births will have to equal (a) the Replaced Initial Births, (b) the Replaced Active Population, (c) the Increment to the Replaced Initial Births, and (d) Increments to the Active Population.

The births that replace the Inertial Population and its increment will die during the Current Cycle.

The births which replace the Initial Active Population and its increment will remain alive during the Current Cycle.

All the births of the Current Cycle thus clone the Initial Population and adds an increment consisting of Increment to Initial Inertial Births and Increment to Initial Active Population. The upshot is that the Effective Population (all births during the Current Cycle), when added to the Initial Population, yields a construction that creates the total population, equal to (a) twice the Initial Population, plus (b) an Increment to the Initial Population.

The past (Initial Population) is preserved in the present (Effective Population), with a pathway (Incremental Population) pointing towards the future. Hence, the future Effective Population should be construed as the Current Effective Population, plus an increment dictated by the upcoming new Current Cycle of the ensuing 100 years.

The most recent 100 years, which define the Current Cycle, accounts for the hard-wiring of every segment of the population into a time-framework. Mimicking Table 2.1, the time-framework is divided vertically into two major parts—the period from year 1 to year T-100 (Initial Period), and the period from year T-99 to year T (the Current Cycle).

The Current Cycle uses the most recent 100 years of birthing. For computational purposes, we have used the same time frame for the Reproduced Initial Population as that for the Initial Population. The Total Population can then be computed as the sum of (a) twice the Initial Population plus (b) the Increment to the Initial Population.

This double-dipping is not just a computational stunt. It signifies the fact that the change over from one cycle to the next incorporates into the movement both a constant velocity and a linear velocity. The constant velocity is in the change from the Initial Population to the Cloned Initial Population.

At the same time, the Incremental change represents a positive or negative growth of the Initial Population.

The 100-year duration is required because every individual member of the population is biologically scheduled to succumb to death at some age between zero and 99 years. Thus, a cycle of this magnitude defines the minimum number of years in which the population can reproduce itself. Such a cycle can then be repeated continuously every year thereafter.

The Current Year is a moving feast; every new year of birth automatically becomes the first year of a new cycle. The activities that take place during the 100-year cycle are mimicked during any one of its component years.

It should be noted that despite the 100-year constraint, population activities during the Current Cycle still depend on births that took place throughout the past life of the population. At the first year of the Current Cycle, the population is faced with the existence of the Initial Population, consisting of all births from year 1 to the beginning of the Current Cycle. Two sub-groups make up this initial population. They are Inertial Births (dead members) and Active Population (living members).

The starting activity of the new cycle is the cloning of the Initial Population with new births. Some of the new births will succumb to death during this cycle; the others will survive during this cycle. This is the minimum task that the population faces at the beginning of the Current Cycle. It must maintain the initial quantitative level of the population, while also preserving its mortality structure. The Initial Inertial Births will be born and will die during the Current Cycle; the Initial Active Population, however, will die and will be born and remain alive within the Current Cycle.

A powerful conclusion can be drawn from these events. Death of the active population, whose members were born in the previous Cycle, is the voice that commands the population to produce births during the current cycle. This makes possible a link-up of the present with the past. Repetition of this action from year to year creates an unbroken chain of births from the distant past into the indefinite future.

On the other hand, the source of births that made the Replaced Inertial Population during the Current Cycle is part of the births commanded by the death of the Active Population discussed in the previous paragraph. These births will also die within the Current Cycle. They will thus be reproduced as the same mortality status as they were at the beginning of the cycle. Birth and death in the Current cycle describes this segment of the population.

Some of the births that made the Replaced Active Population during the Current Cycle will survive. They are reproduced as the same mortality status as they were at the beginning of the cycle.

The Replaced Initial Population, with its associated births and deaths, define the replacement function of population activity. It is the process that insures the preservation of the past quantitative attribute of the population from year to year throughout the current cycle and even from cycle to cycle.

In summary, the Effective Population consists of all births during the Current Cycle. They are the products of the Initial Active Population, whose death during the Current Cycle created the need. They replace the Initial Population in quantity and mortality configuration. They also provide an increment thereto.

The catch phrase here is: "some deaths in the present determine all births in the present; some births in the present determine some deaths in the present".

Death morphs into birth; both birth and death, on the other hand, morph into death. This mortality temporal dance during the Current Cycle insures the stability in numbers and mortality structure of the population. It may even provide for future growth of the population.

Some of the properties of time set critical constraints on population formation. In describing Table 2.1 we only mentioned in passing the outer frames. The outer frames are of critical importance and need to be described in some detail. We also need a picture of the background structure of the time frames.

An individual birth takes place during the Current Year within a family led by two adult parents. But this birth is not a lonesome act. It is accompanied by a group of births during that year, each within its own family. The population trail begins by encasing all births during the Current Year within a Quantum Cocoon. This will be their home for the duration of their lives.

With the passage of each year, it appears that time is moving by one unit. We hypothesize in this work that the motion involved is being done by the Quantum Cocoon. It is a process in which time is standing unchanged, while the Cocoon is moving up its stationary left frame and down its stationary right frame at one unit per year.

We postulate that time is a stationary object, akin to a ladder, with two parallel vertical side frame, joined together by horizontal rungs of two sections—left and right. The rungs are equally calibrated in one-year units of time. Each unit of time is divided into two sections.

The vertical frames are continuous. On the left side the markers point upward; on the right side they point downward.

The length along the vertical sides is indeterminate.

The left half of the frame is laying on a subset of earth matter which we designate as human earth matter. The right half of the frame is lying on a subset of earth matter which we designate as non-human earth matter.

In summary, the time frame is grounded in the earth. It unites two subsets of earth matter, with opposite but complementary attributes. It unites them to form a time frame within which the population can create its members and the materials necessary for their creation and development. Out of the earth the population member will experience his beginning of time; into the earth such member will experience his end of time.

Each year of birth, t, on the left side is joined with a companion integer, r, on the right side. The integer, r, is the age during the Current Year of births. It is identically, r = (T-t), the difference between the Current Year and the year of birth.

The right side is reserved for descending time units with r, going from 0 to (T-1). The left side is reserved for ascending time units with t going from 1 to T.

These two opposite time scales complete the connection between the start of the upward direction from year 1 to the Current year, T, together with the descent from age 0, to its end at age (T-1).

The apparent flow of time from its origin to its peak, then downward from its peak back to its destiny, is an illusion. Time is stationary; the motion is engendered by the ascending births, with every new annual incremental Quantum Cocoon, q(T), of birth, coming into being and occupying a vacant position at the top of the fixed time-frame, on the left-hand side. Simultaneously, the motion is engendered by the changing descending pattern of age, with every new incremental quantum of age, q(r), coming into being and occupying its vacant position in the time frame, on the right-hand side.

All these motions of the various quanta of births give the appearance of time moving in lock-step fashion with the actual movements of births.

Table 2.1 below depicts a segment of a birthing scheme. The slots in the time frame reserved for every Quantum Cocoon that has been forming for six years. The last column depicts the birthing pattern for all six years.

The previous five columns detail the year by year process of creating a new quantum of birth. As the new quantum of birth is added, note that every one of the slots add one year of age to its age the previous year.

The remarkable result of the emergence of a new quantum of birth, q(T), is that it generates a pattern of birth and age, q(T) = q(t,r), for every specific pair, (t,r), during the current year. Each position in the time frame has a unique pair of identifiers, (t,r). These two numbers are related by the identity that age, r, is the difference between the Current year, T, and the year of birth, t; that is, r = (T-t).

The series below gives a symbolic statement of the apparent flow of time. The series, t, of specific year of birth is the left-hand upward units of the time-frame. The series, r, of specific age during the Current year is the right-hand downward units of time of the time-frame. The sum of the two companion identifiers is identically equal to the Current Year. During the current year, the incremental crop of births, q(T) = q(t) + q(r), attaches the quantum of birth to the top of the time frame. What is remarkable is that the same current quantum of birth is the specific increment of birth of every specific year of birth in the population.

The population time frame selects two opposite forms of earth matter—human and non-human--to enclose the creative activities of the Effective Population membership. Out of non-human earth matter it starts the process in motion by creating its members; it then rears them by enabling them to use non-human earth matter to maintain their lives, to develop them, to hone their attributes, and finally to send them to their end, back into their place of destiny in the realm of non-human earth matter.

The following definitions summarize the description of the two vertical time frames, (t,r), and the births they carry on each unit of time.

t=1, 2, 3,...,(T-2),(T-1),(T);
r=(T-1), (T-2, (T-3),...,2, 1, 0.
T = t+r.
q(T) = q(t) + q(r).

The quantum of births during the Current year is identically equal to the sum of the quantum of births and its companion quantum of age.

For every specific year of birth, the sum of the year of birth and the age equals the Current year. It follows that the incremental quantum of birth during the current year is the same quantum for every one of the specific year of birth.

This consequence of the time-frame structure is mind-boggling. For each upward unit of time, it calculates the companion year of age during the Current year. What it does is to enable anyone during the Current year to observe a snapshot of the history of the origin and all the annual steps in the formation of the population which took place over the life of the population. It is as if hundreds of years of population activities are collapsed into one year.

Finally, we indicate some of the implications of how the time-frame distinguishes between the behavior of one individual population member compared to the activities of groups of population members cooperatively executing a specific population reproducing task.

Individual population behavior is identified with a specific year within a specific span of years. Such a year is the Current Year, T(t,r), which is associated with every unique pair, (t,r), of identifiers.

This means that at the same time, each birth year cohort can be performing tasks that differ from those of any other of its birth year cohort. This may lead to the false conclusion that the same individual can perform many different tasks at the same time in many different locations. The different individuals involved appear to be one and same in the sense that they carry the same pair of identifiers, (t,r).

On the other hand, the performance of a population activity is a function of an aggregate of population members from different birth year groups within specific contiguous blocks of years of birth. Every item in Table 2.2 indicates the important blocks of time required for the creation of a population from the activities of cooperating groups of population members.

The impact of this description of the population time-frame is enormous. It is an architectural birthing plan from which a population may be constructed. But more important, it provides an observational instrument with which to confront reality to disprove descriptive hypotheses concerning population outcomes.

From the vantage point of the Current year, it enables the analyst to observe the annual history of the birthing operation of a population. Activities which took place a great many years in the past become a snapshot in the Current year of the present.

And lastly, some consequences of the nature of the time-frame make clear an otherwise strange attribute of population formation.

Every population member has a specific year of birth. At the time of birth, the year of birth is also the Current year. This means that it is a year specific to a set of individuals, yet it is simultaneously, the common birth year of every specific birth year group. It is simultaneously social and individual. All this means that every individual has a personal identity, but he also belongs to a Cocoon in the social grouping called a population.

Not to worry. The individual so conflicted still has a unique identity, T(t,r) during the new current year. When he was born his year of birth was the Current and his identity was T(T,0); his age during the year of his birth was 0. But what of the next incremental year of birth, and the next, and so on.

One year after its birth, a new quantum of births occupies the new birth position, T(T,0), which did not exist before. The position that he and his cohorts now have maintained the year of birth, t, as before; however, it is now one year prior to the new Current Year T. Therefore, it is designated as t = T-1; it's magnitude has not changed. It's former T-name is now stated as a member of the specific year of birth series, and not now a Current Year, T.

What has changed for the identity of the former occupant of the Current Year is the age identity. It has acquired an incremental year of age. Its identity is now T(t,1), where t has the same value as before, but the new Current Year, T, is now one year greater than the previous year.

This circumstance is true for every specific year of birth identity. No change is experienced here for an increment of birth. But every one of these identities experiences a one year increment in age.

Please consult Table 2.1 above for a demonstration of these events if it appears to be too complex. From the table you will note that for every change in the Current Year, any specific year of birth remains the same. This is seen by moving in a horizontal direction. At the same time, the series of year of birth moves upward; the series of age move downward; and the Current Year moves in an upward sloping direction.

Let us note that the specific year of birth is nothing but the year of the start of Life. It never changes. Every year from then on upward to the Current year, is a year of survival of the Quantum Cocoon. The same downward span of years is the years of death of those Quantum Cocoons.

During any span years, beginning with a specific year of birth and ending with the Current Year, a specific quantum of birth travels up the span in a life-survival mode; simultaneously, this same specific quantum journeys downward within the same span on the approach toward the end of life.

The motion of every quantum of birth, during any given span of years, accompanies such a quantum with an ever-changing identity. The time frame remains fixed, so the year of birth remains fixed; movement of the quantum increases from the year of birth to the Current year in yearly increments; the age of the quantum also increases downward from the Current year to its age during the Current Year in yearly increments.

Let us interpret the age during the Current year to mean the years of completed life to date. Every year of birth from the Current year downward to the age during the Current year is nothing but an additional year towards the end of life.

For the individual, it is now clear that the Current Year is the year of life. Ascending time-frame years for the individual are years of survival. So, too, descending time frame years are years of death, of life coming to end.

Life, then, for the individual is a dynamic synthesis of its opposites—birth and age. The population activity that unites them is congealed in the Current Year, T.

For the population, the Current Year is the Year of Birth. The aggregate number of years of birth going upward to the Current Year are years of survival. Similarly, the aggregate number of years going downward over the same span of years as the companion years of survival are the years of death.

In the case of the population, then, the aggregation of individual lives is the dynamic synthesis of its opposites—aggregate years of birth and aggregate years of age. The synthesis that unites them is aggregate Births, measured by the aggregation of Quantum Cocoons of the Current Year over the span of years of population formation.

Another property of time is that each of its units carries a specific quantum, $q(T) = q(t) + q(r)$, of births of discrete human population members. This moving quantum is exactly the sum of the Velocity of Survival plus the Velocity of Death.

We want to repeat what we have learned thus far that the Velocity of Birth during the Current Year yields an observable cross-section history of the joint distribution of the velocity of every unique $Q(T) = q(t) + q(r)$, Velocity of Year of Birth and its associated Velocity of Age during the Current year. During one special year, the Current Year, we can empirically observe the operation of population formation activities which took place during every year in the life of the population.

This is mind-boggling. The time constraint on population formation makes it possible to get a snapshot of the past population formation and development during the current year. It also gives us similar real time observation of what part of the future development will be like. Assuming that the development path of the past will be followed in the future, we now have a plausible indication of the entire history of the population, from genesis day to the day of demise.

The temporal skeletal structure of births of population members consists of two groups of opposing but complementary years. The year of birth starts at year 1 and ends with the current year, T. The reverse is age during the current year, starting at age 0 during Current Year and ending with the oldest age at year T-1.

Since time is continuous, the birthing process can begin a new cycle during any given year. We then have that whenever a specific year of birth is the Current Year it is the carrier of a new Quantum Cocoon of births of discrete new population members. As a new year occurs the quantum of births which is carried by that year becomes the common increment of births for every specific annual birth group. At the same time, every specific birth group rations its incremental birth membership among its living and its dead.

The empirical meaning of these postulates is that the number of surviving population members associated with each specific year of birth is the aggregate of births which survived the period starting from the specific year of birth and ending with the current year. At the same time, the age of any specific birth year group is the span of deaths among all the births during the reverse interval of these same years.

Numerically, these two span of years are identically equal; the aggregate births within each span, however, are unequal; likewise, the sum of the Velocities of Surviving Births and its companion Velocity of Deaths is unequal.

The result of the partition of births into living and dead is a structure of the population birthing process in which each specific year of birth is stamped with a pair of identifiers-- specific year of birth and specific age during the current year. When in motion along a path of a span of years, their meaning change to years of survival and accompanying years of death. These two numbers sum identically to the current year. Thus, births and deaths within the population are two phases of the same birthing activity, taking place simultaneously but having opposite but complementary effects.

The Current Year is the year of birth for the population and is therefore commonly owned by each specific year of birth. But as a pair the specific year of birth and its corresponding age during the Current Year are unique to the specific Quantum Cocoon of that year.

Every individual member of the population originates within a family. It came bundled in a Cocoon with a number of fellow birth mates, every one of which carries the same ID, T(t,r).

This is a very important fact to keep in mind. The families who gave birth to the same ID cohorts are the current subset of adults in the age group, ranging between 16 and 50 years of age. Their number is as large as the number of individuals in the birth quantum, differing because of the number of multiple births during the year of birth. They reside throughout the entire geographical area occupied by the population.

These families carry out their responsibilities of birthing their members; of maintaining the lives of these members; of developing and honing the attributes of these members; of disposing of the remains of these members on occasion of their deaths.

The significant point is that the cohorts in the quantum of birth can be in the millions. At the same time, the number of families that gave birth to them is likewise in the millions, located in an area the size of the national political state in which they reside. Their individual members, under the supporting mechanisms of the families, go about their business of living, exercising their own choices of activities, times of performing these activities, locations in which they will do their tasks, and a host of other actions apparently dictated by individual choice.

It is no mystery why an astute observer, who does not possess the appropriate time-framework to capture the behaviors of individual family members, may see the same ID carrying out these many different activities at different times in different locations, with different velocities.

He may then conclude that the family structure condones other-worldly attributes of its membership.

The effect on the family of the temporal birthing structure is very crucial. The family is the institution within which the birth of the population member takes place. It is also the institution in which the individual will have its life maintained and in which it will develop and hone its individual attributes.

An individual member will pass through many stages of development until it reaches the age of maturity. It may then choose to desert the family and assume the responsibilities of parenting a new family. It may also choose to live as an independent single-member family.

Along the way, the member may die and that will seem to end its existence and any tangible effects that it may have on the family from which it departed. However, it will still leave the imprint of its age on its surviving birth cohorts. That imprint will have some significant effect on the way in which the population will move within its future time framework.

The constraints of time and of parental birthing of new population members suggests that the constraint of family activities plays a fundamental role in determining population formation and development.

Family as Arena for Births and Maintenance of Life

Every birthing activity depends upon the bonding of two separate and distinct adult members of the population. The coming together of these adults is not a fortuitous event. Indeed, it is circumscribed by a host of institutional constraints originating out of the historical experiences of the population members as a highly specialized organism with a life of its own, independent of any one of its individual constituent members. Among other things, these constraints are intertwined with mores and values concerning acquaintanceship among young people, courtship, marriage, family formation, family function, family dissolution, and a host of other behavioral restrictions.

The family is the arena in which the birthing activity is conducted. Indeed, it is the core unit, the cell, the atom of the population. Within it, pairs of adult individuals make decisions to produce the babies who ultimately form the foundation stones of the population. At the same time, the family inherits the task of maintaining the lives and development of all its members.

First and foremost, it harbors two adults. On some occasions, as a member of a subset of fertile families, it may give birth to a new baby. In each ensuing year, a different subset of families will engage in birthing, thus making possible the uninterrupted sequence of annual injections of new baby crops into the population membership pool.

During its lifetime, a randomly chosen adult parent pair will give birth a certain number of times. This number is subject to a distribution, varying from zero to a relatively small number of cases. This is a very critical datum for the population of which the family is a part. It is usually referred to as the average size family We would expect this number to remain fairly stable over a long period of years.

Most families produce a single birth in a given year of birthing. In a relatively few cases some families produce twins, or triplets, or quadruplets, or even higher multiple births. It follows that the number of families who give birth to a quantum of births in any given year is almost as great as the number of babies in that quantum. The difference is relatively small, by less than the number of multiple births that year. In a known case in recent years, the number of families was in the neighborhood of four million families; the incidence of multiple births was less than seven thousand.

The members of the population, as well as the members of every family, are distributed among all age groups from 0 to 99 years of age. At the lowest age are the babies born during the current year. Above them are the children, ranging in age between 1 and 15 years old. The children, including the new born babies, are highly dependent on their parents for support and maintenance of their lives.

The next higher rung consists of young adults, ranging from age 16 to 49 years of age. This group is very special. Its constituents are generally biologically capable of participating as parents in the birthing of children. At the lower end, however, they will still be highly dependent on their parents for living support.

These are followed by older adults, ranging from 50 to 99 years of age. This group is the elderly who may now be biologically incapable of creating children, but who may still play an active role as head or assistants to the heads of families.

These various age groups can be identified with activities which are peculiar to their group within their respective families and in the population at large. But whatever the distinction, the age-related functions are cogent mementos of the burden of maintaining the living status of the family members. At the same time, the birth-related functions are cogent mementos of the growth, development, and honing the attributes of the family members' lives.

The age structure of the family is a microcosm of the age structure of the population. The difference is that the family age structure has many missing age slots. The ageing pathway mirrors and reflects all activities by which every family member progresses in stages from birth to death. The life of the individual within the family, like the existing age-structure of the population, starts from birth, goes through a childhood stage, passes into adulthood, and finally achieves potential longevity. Along the way, at every age, some of these family members succumb to death and depart from playing an active role in population reproduction activities. However, we shall see that they still play a necessary part in enabling the population to transcend the barriers of time.

The age structure of the family members is an image of the extent of annual decay of the corresponding annual births. It is a potent view of the quantitative burden of maintaining the lives of the population members.

This dual function of the family birthing activity immediately gives us an unambiguous understanding of the meaning of the Current Year.

During the Current year, the span of time beginning with the year of birth and ending in the Current Year is an exact measure of the number of years of life currently experienced by each member of any given birth year group. Similarly, during the Current Year, the age of these births measures the number of years of life completed to date. These two span of years are equal to each other, with each pointing in opposite directions.

It is interesting to note that changes in the time-related attributes of the individuals are tied to the span of years during the interval of motion. On the other hand, changes in the population made by a group of individuals are tied to the aggregate of years during the interval of motion. This is a most important distinction.

What this amounts to is that an aggregate result within a given time span is the total for the population during that span. On the other hand, the change in the aggregate relative to the size of the span is the Velocity of the element undergoing change. For example, the quantum of births, q(T), is the Velocity of Births for the population. It is indeed the increment of births in the population corresponding to an increment of one year in time. Aggregating this quantum over any time span yields the population during that span of years in which the aggregation took place.

For the population, any incremental births during the Current Year increases the age of every year of birth by one year. At the same time, every member of the population experiences an increment of one year of life.

Empirical observation of families will display a random collection of members by age groups. The age groups of every family, like that of the population, will be between zero and 99. The family distribution will exhibit many gaps, however, since family births will be limited to a range from 1 to 5, with few exceptions, going as high as 20.

Finally, no two-family members will have the same age. This will only occur in case of multiple births during a given year. While such random observation may seem a bit daunting, we note at once that both the year of birth and the age during the Current Year of any family member are tightly related to the Current Year. The sum of these two identifying quantities is identically equal to the Current Year.

The year of birth of a population member is simply the year of start of life of that member. At the same time, the age of such member during the Current Year is the years of completed lifetime to date. Hence the Current Year is the year of life of the individual--the synthesis of its start of life and its end of life to date. It is indeed a common year of life for every population member. Each surviving population member has the dual attribute of year of birth and age during the Current Year. Any specific year of birth group therefore possesses a unique pair of these two attributes, distinct from any other birth year group.

The age attribute is the difference between the Current Year and the year of birth, in the reverse direction. This is likewise identically equal to the years of life achieved by each specific birth year group during the Current Year. We can now hypothesize that the age attribute of each population member is a mark that symbolizes the connection to death of any member of a surviving population birth year group. It is therefore possible that a census of Active Population members can give us a way of determining the distribution of dead members and the temporal pattern of their demise. After all, the age is an attribute of every population member. Therefore, it is directly related to the death attribute of every surviving population member.

Since the family is embedded in the population the observations of the previous paragraph are true for the family.

Appropriate aggregations of year of birth and age during the Current Year, and other quantitative and non-quantitative data for each member within each family for a Current Year, will yield a set of significant information that represents the real world population. The aggregates of interest to us are those which will simulate the process by which population members originate, how they bond together to form a population, how the population maintains itself and grows over time, and how it comes to end.

Individual Activities of Family Members

An individual population member goes about his daily tasks as an independent operative, distinct from all his acquaintances. He behaves as if he were the same as they are as a human being. But he also believes that he is his own man, independently making his own choices to do what he must do to live his life as he sees fit. We know better than he that he is a creature of a birthing relationship, which takes place within the confines of a specific family, among a group of families in the same population of which he is a member.

His family is one of as many as the number of distinct individuals in his Quantum Cocoon of birth. These families are scattered throughout the geographic domain in which the population resides. They are members of clans of kinship families, of groups of clans, of various combinations of groups of clans. They pay obedience to a political state which operates on a variety of levels—national, state, and local government jurisdictions. Within these jurisdictions, they are members of various groups, of school districts, of water districts, of counties, of cities, of villages, of states, and numerous other governmental bodies.

The occasion of a person's birth places him within a very specific cell within the population framework from whence he will execute his survival activities from year of birth, through the stages of childhood, young adulthood, old age, and death. He may succumb somewhere in one of those stages before achieving potential longevity. Nevertheless, his survival requires the support of his family to make possible whatever survival he may achieve.

His entire existence will place him in a time-frame cell with an id, T(t,r), which only he and his birth cohorts enjoy. The initial cell maintains its unique year of birth status. As a new Current Year of birth takes place this signifies that the population, the families that make it up, and the individual members of those families are in motion in a mode of formation and development. The age during the Current Year id changes in conformity.

When a new Current Year slot is occupied by a new crop of babies, some of the denizens of each previously existing slot acquire one slot downward, for a total of T-1 slots downward. The new members of the year of birth set acquire one new slot upward. This is the underlying dynamic of a population. It demands the exact placement of every individual in its reserved position in the time-frame of its organized activities.

To start the task of simulating the role of the family, we must place the family in the time-frame in consonance with the placement each of its members. We must first assemble the two adult members of the family who have satisfied the mores governing family formation. They form a family, consisting of themselves at this juncture. They then engage jointly in the birthing activity and produce a baby, which is a distinct addition to the family and therefore to the population.

This new baby must now be placed in the correct slot of the population time-framework. In such a position, it will occupy the right slot within which it can join with others to perform the population activities characteristic of that cooperative slot.

His position is inviolate. It is, at the time of birth, uniquely identified by T(t,r). To place him requires us to place the quantum, q(T) = q(T) + q(0). This quantum is a unique one of all other quanta, q(T) = q(t) +q(r).

But this baby belongs to one family; and all his birth cohorts likewise belong to several families, equal in number to his birth cohorts. Each of these families has its own version of a distribution of year of birth, (t), and age, (r). Slotting one baby requires slotting all cohort families in the same slot, (T,0), the one reserved for the current quantum of births, at the top of the population time-frame.

This is done by vertically overlaying the appropriate Current Year of birth slot with all families, pivoted on a descending path of the birth year. This procedure should capture all members of all Current birth year families in their reserved slots in the time-framework.

Similarly, we must also place these families horizontally, pivoting them on the age ID. This allows for the proper placement of these families on all age slots that other members of their families should occupy.

Table 2.2 gives an example of how this positioning of a new member of the population is consummated. It involves slotting the entire quantum of births of this member in the slot reserved for the Current Year, taking due account of the constraints of family on population formation.

The procedure which we have outlined above relates to Active Population members only. We have no way of slotting the dead members. All is not lost, however. Each surviving member carries a scar of death in its age attribute. The aggregate of this attribute over a relevant group of Active Population members is an exact measure of death within that aggregate group.

The problem of placing the quantum of birth in its reserved cell in the population time-frame is a rather easy one to solve. The apparent complication arises from the fact that we had to simultaneously slot all other members of the birth year families. The nature of the time frame made it a fairly simple task.

The members of any quantum of births are the newest members of the population. Every newborn possesses his own distinct form as well as degree of dependence on his parents. At birth the problem of maintaining his life and developing and honing his attributes begins in earnest. Much of these activities by individuals are age-related. However, some are so necessary that they must be carried out by every member of the population.

Food consumption comes to mind as the first and most important activity. Food is the elixir of life. It has to be ingested into the body day in and day out in the life of every individual. Without it one would succumb to death. Food is the agent whose consumption is transformed into human energy. It is the life-sustaining manna from heaven.

Food comes in a number of different types, is eaten in various dietary combinations, at different venues, and at different times of the day, by different individuals. It is eaten at home, away from home, in fast food places, in posh steak houses, in fast food joints. It is served as Chinese, Thai, Greek, Italian. It comes in the form of vegan diets, Mediterranean diets, soul food diets.

The critical fact in all this is that each individual behaves as an independent actor, exercising choices, and generally behaving as if he were a completely free agent. The truth is that these individuals are all subject to constraints of parental birthing and family enclosure.

Food consumption is necessary for the replacement of human energy lost in the act of living. Consumption of other goods provides protection and specific form to the human energy. They provide the receptacle in which the human energy is held, the physical mass of the energy, the inertial property of the energy, the dead weight of the energy.

Foremost among these non-food items is housing. This is absolutely necessary to provide a central place for the family to function, to carry out its major activities. It must have a place for the birthing activity. It must have a place for sleep, an interval of time in which the transformation of food into human energy takes place; a time in which energy is not being expended, but is being absorbed.

Housing comes in a variety of forms. Single family homes, apartments, condominiums, boats on a river, penthouses are a few possibilities.

Clothing, personal care, health care are consumed by all individuals. Like other consumer goods, they come in endless varieties. They are highly age-related. They also come in various styles with the changing times.

A most important agent of consumption is schooling. In the childhood years population members may be subject to kindergarten, elementary, and junior high schooling. Young adults may partake of high school, college, professional, and graduate training. Older members may even partake of various types of unlimited schooling.

Other important consumption activities involve recreation, entertainment, communication, transportation.

To obtain these consumer goods in a capitalist society one must acquire them by giving up a sum of money. The source of money, at least for the wage working class, is money wages. Parents and young adults must negotiate with capitalists to receive wages in exchange for their human energy.

The money wages in turn are used to acquire the consumer goods by giving them to capitalists in exchange for the consumer goods.

These activities of selling and buying are crucial for the heads of families upon whom support is required by young members.

Having received wages, the parents must then go into the capitalists' workplaces and exert their energies to produce the products which they or the capitalists use. Getting to these workplaces and back home, day by day, is an interesting sight to see. By train, plane, bus, ferry, personal automobile the parents go in what seems like an avalanche. Autos on the freeways, interstates, state highways, county roads, speeding in both directions on these arteries in the morning and late afternoon hours, appear to be a non-ending activity.

These are examples of the types of activities in which members of the population are engaged on a daily basis. They appear to be quite random, dependent only on individual choice, and executed for reasons only known to the individual involved.

But these individuals are members of a population. The population requires various collections of its members, poised strategically inside its time-frame, to perform certain population reproducing tasks. The population constraints which it imposes on the family, and therefore, on the population member is the subject of the following chapter.

Population Reproduction Supersedes Family Activity

We have stated elsewhere that population is a special group of people who are locked together in a social embrace undergoing a process of reproduction of themselves to the exclusion of all other people. The fundamental reproductive activity is human labor, exerted in two phases—external and internal—with a periodicity of 100 years. External labor is the activity in which members of the population exert their efforts upon the earth, external to themselves, to produce the material means of their survival. Internal labor is the activity in which population members exert their efforts upon themselves to create and maintain themselves.

The resulting population membership is manifested by the total number of births which took place over the entire period from the genesis of the population up through the current year. This number, in turn, consists of two essential segments—the number of current survivors and the number of dead members. The latter constitutes the inertial factor, the "mass" of the population. These two segments, in dynamic combination, completely describe the quantitative trait of the human population during the current year.

These births come in a long and unbroken temporal series within family units. Each occurrence involves three individuals—two adult parents and one new-born baby. Each of the two adults was the result of a birthing activity sometime in the past. And the parents of these parents are themselves the result of birthing activities further back into the past. Similarly, the baby involved in a current birthing activity will someday join in a birthing activity with another adult population member to generate a future baby; and so on, ad infinitum.

Every member of a population is, was, or will be generated out of a continuing and unbroken sequence of birthing activities from the present, back into the past to the time of the original formation of the population; and forward from the present into the indefinite future to the year of demise of the population.

Population, therefore, is the institution which provides order and purpose to the results of birthing activities by all families combined, over the historical life of the population. It harnesses the freely acting families, installs upon their activities an ordered set of constraints of their behavior which leads to a specific path of future growth and development of the population.

Among other things, the population sets the accumulated base of births from the past as a foundation template within which to imbed the births of the Current Cycle. During the Current Cycle it then "clones" this foundation and, if necessary, adds an increment thereto.

Cloning provides for the continuation of the population at the same quantitative level as before. Replacing the accumulated base is the minimum quantitative task that the population must perform in order that the population persists for another cycle. If it is a growing population it also creates a positive increment; if it is a diminishing population the increment is negative; and finally, if it is a stable population the increment is zero.

Effective Population

We define the Effective Population as that segment of the population which contains all the members who could possibly be alive during the current year. If the maximum number of years of life of any member is designated as "potential longevity", then the Effective Population consists of all members who were born during the period equal in years to potential longevity, where such a period includes the current year and the requisite number of years preceding the current year. In short, it includes all population members who are of an age between zero and potential longevity during the Current Year.

The Effective Population is the core of the entire population. In a seed-like manner it generates all the population reproducing activities. Some of its members are alive and some are dead. Thereby, it inheres an organic composition which should reflect the organic composition of the population as a whole.

The Effective Population is indeed the heart of the entire population. It beats in obedient rhythmic response to the constant tempo of the passage of time, consistent with the systematic carrying out of its essential activities by its collective membership.

As the Current Year passes out of existence and is succeeded by a new current year, the oldest adults quit the environs of the Effective Population and take their places among the members of the past generations. Simultaneously, the oldest members of the younger adults move up in the hierarchy of the Effective Population. At the same time, the oldest children shed their childhood integuments to become active adults. Correspondingly, some otherwise future members take their places in the roles of a brand new crop of babies within the effective population.

The result is that part of the Effective Population becomes an integral part of the past generations; part of the future generations joins the fold of the Effective Population; and the internal composition of the Effective Population undergoes an annual change of some of the individuals who make up its membership, and possibly also undergoes a change in the number of members as well as a change in the distribution of members' traits. And all of this is done in precision-stepping to the unvarying tempo of the passage of a year's time.

If now we consider the passage of an interval of time equal to potential longevity, rather than the passage of one year, it then follows that the entire initial effective population has now moved on to occupy a position among the past generations. Its former place is currently usurped by a brand new Effective Population whose membership originated out of the future generations. The dynamical result is that the future generations come to life to replenish the present generations, which have faded into the past generations. The accomplishment of all of this has been made possible by the birthing activities and by the life-destroying activities, in conjunction with all the other essential population activities, over the specified time interval. The old membership disappears; a new set of members refreshes the vacated environs, thereby preserving the existence and vitality of the Effective Population.

It is as if the entire population undergoes a pulsating internal metamorphosis. At the core o-f the population is the Effective Population, churning with the activities of its members in a frenzy of intersecting motions. The phase of contraction reflects the playing out of the life-times of the members in the form of deaths. The expanding phase corresponds to the enlarging of the core as the future generations refresh the population through the birthing activity. And finally, the dynamic balancing of the two phases of expansion and contraction symbolize the resultant creation of a brand new Effective Population.

Nothing in the preceding set of events precludes their repetition over the next succeeding effective period; nor over the effective period following the latter, and so on and on over a long succession of effective periods. The major point here is that the underlying temporal pattern of births and the inherent temporal pattern of deaths which drives the former, in coordination with all the other essential activities, play the decisive roles in dictating the membership and characteristic signature of the effective population over exceedingly long periods of time.

The current Effective Population originates out of the past; the same forces which created it will generate the future Effective Population out of the present. Past and future thus form the basis for a synthesis which is the present.

Population Arithmetic

The quantitative data supplied by the real world population are derivable from the aggregation of family birth and related data during the current year. A well-designed census of families is one engine for such aggregation. An integral source of other real data is the maintenance of registries of births, deaths, and related data over the course of years. The combination of all these efforts yields some critical material for testing descriptive hypotheses concerning population formation.

Our conception of the structure of the population is shown in Table 2.1 at the beginning of this chapter.

It consists of three major segments—Initial Population, Effective Population, and Total Population.

Initial Population is composed of all births prior to the Current Cycle. It consists of two subs-groups—Initial Active Population and Initial Inertial Population.

Effective Population consists of all births during the Current Cycle. It encompasses two sub-groups—Cloned Initial Population and Incremental Initial Population.

The third group is simply the sum of the preceding two. It is the Total Population.

The general formula we discovered for estimating these population segments is contained in the following:

P = bT^2 plus or minus 50bT;
Where P is Population, b is a constant, T is Current Year.

Using the subtracting element yields the Initial Population; using the addition element yields the Effective Population. Adding the Initial Population to the Effective Population yields the Total Population.

This is quite an interesting, simple, and compact formula. It says that the Total Population is composed of two Initial Populations, plus the Increment to the Initial Population.

The formula contains the constant, b. This is a constant of acceleration. If it is applicable, then the motion of the population entails a combination of linear velocity, constant velocity, and zero velocity. A detailed discussion of this parameter is reserved for a later chapter.

Of immediate interest is the estimation of the two critical components in a Population—Active Population and Inertial Births. Active Population is the surviving segment; Inertial Births are the dead component.

For the case of the Effective Population, the formulas of estimation are:

Active Population = 0.5bT^2 + 0.5bT
Inertial Births = 49.5bT

During the current reproduction cycle the population accumulates the births that took place more than one hundred years ago. This process of accumulation is the preparation of a mold, suitably positioned, in which to imbed the current births. This amounts to setting the past birthing activity as a foundation for launching future births. The current births must have a predetermined match from the past to which it will be meshed during the current cycle. Every birth must be mated with a corresponding dead population member who was born previous to the current cycle.

Once the task of accumulation is completed successfully the birthing activity of the Current Cycle is then able to generate an increment of births above or below the level of the Initial Births.

This is heady stuff. We are postulating here that the process of formation of population membership by the birthing activity can be completely described with the use of one parameter, the rate of births (the change in the velocity of births divided by the corresponding change in the years of birth). This is the unique factor. Its determination and application will provide a critical comparison with some real world descriptors of U.S. population formation in later chapters.

We have traversed a long and torturous path from an individual life of a population member, created by a special binary operation involving an adult male and an adult female, in the arena of a family institution which they head. We enclosed the birth into a Quantum Cocoon, binding together all the births of the Current Year of birth. We then imposed a time-frame ID upon this Cocoon (and therefore on all its cohorts). The ID consisted of two markers—year of birth and age during the Current Year.

Using the ID to organize all the births into a pliable form, we aggregated individual live births to form an Active Population and a set of Inertial Births—two essential groups of births which stand at the strategic readiness to engage in the creative acts of Human Labor to reproduce the population and its non-human means of survival.

The next few chapters will try to clarify this trail of creation and constraints, and to further elucidate the remaining social and physical restraints which impinge upon those single individuals who are the ultimate base units of populations.

3

Human Labor

WE HAVE COME a long way. Our path started with one individual life. We followed it through the life of a living individual as a result of a binary operation involving its parents in a family setting.

We saw it encased in a Quantum Cocoon of annual births. This brought it into a tightly intertwined relationship with all the families of that birth cocoon. It also became linked with all the families of the birth cocoons of the family's parents and of the family's other members.

The birth and activities of family members represent a collection of individuals in independent and consciously self-directed movements. What is lacking is a command to impose order and social cohesion to these acts of individual anarchy. This is the role of a social force, of a uniting bond, that sends commands to certain aggregations of ordered births to perform specific population formation activities.

The strategic principle of action is to create a reproductive engine, a mechanism by which the population reproduces itself. The activity for carrying out this task is Human Labor.

Human Labor is the cement that forges a social union that ties together the disparate acts of the many births into one human population. Human Labor makes effective use of individual lives, organized annually within Quantum Cocoons, within family units, inside a time-frame, and aggregated into strategic groups, standing in ready formation to perform population reproduction activities. These groups are sent into a set of purposive actions which result in the formation of a population, distinct from the individual, or its parents, or its family.

Some Important Labor Elements

In order to get a grip on the meaning of Human Labor there are certain aggregations of births that enter into the labor activity that one must be aware of. In addition, one should appreciate what an activity really is.

Here are two definitions which we will be using in this chapter.

Effective Population
= Active Population + Inertial Births

Non-human Matter
= Consumer Goods + Inertial Matter

Effective Population is the total number of births during the Current Cycle. During that cycle the births evolve into two distinct groups—Active Population and Inertial Births. The Active Population is the surviving births; the Inertial Births are the Non-survivors.

Non-Human Matter is the total amount of non-human goods produced during the Current Cycle. During that cycle the goods evolve into two types—Consumer Goods and Inertial Matter. The Consumer Goods are the personally consumable non-human matter, including food. Inertial Matter are non-human goods that are not personally consumable.

Another definition that is crucial for understanding Human Labor is what we mean by an "activity".

We define an activity by parsing it into its five basic components. These are (1) predicate, (2) subject, (3) instrument, (4) object, (5) result and restarter.

The predicate is the activity itself. The subject is the person performing the activity. The instrument is the thing used by the subject to execute the activity. The object is the thing into which the activity is directed. The result is the changed state of the object as a consequence of the activity. The result should also include a restarter of a new cycle of the activity.

This definition makes the activity a self-contained entity, with its ending and beginning merging to make possible its continuation into the future.

To fix ideas, consider a predicate which is the razing of a wall by a group of men in order to build an alternative structure in its place. The subject is the group of men. The instrument is a wrecking ball. The object is the wall. The result is the destroyed wall, together with the removal of the debris.

Human Labor is the activity that uses groups of births as the subject for reproducing a population. At the same time, Human Labor creates and reproduces the non-human means of survival of the population. But it does more that; it accomplishes these tasks in repeated cycles over a long period of time.

This dual function of Human Labor is to be kept in mind. It is more than population reproduction.

Because it exceeds population reproduction it may even create different types of populations, depending upon the set of rules governing how the labor is performed. These rules may dictate the types of non-earth materials to be jointly reproduced, the nature of the auxiliary institutions necessary to perform the labor, the division of the human actors into different classes, the historical era in which the reproduction is taking place, the impact of outside populations on the population in question.

Human Labor functions as two opposing, but complementary, phases—Internal Labor and External Labor.

Internal Labor is the activity which transforms non-human earth material means of survival into human earth material. External Labor is the activity which transforms human earth material into non-human earth material.

These two phases of Labor are assisted by two auxiliary sets of institutions—a set of synthesizing conduits of the Instruments of Labor which link up the two phases of Internal and External Labor; and a set of analytic processes which accumulate the objects of Labor.

The conduits consist of two partners. One conduit enables the passage of the instrument of External Labor from Internal Labor to External Labor. The other conduit enables the passage of the instrument of Internal Labor from External Labor to Internal Labor. These conduits therefore provide for the link-up of both phases of Human Labor.

It is important to note that the instrument of one type of labor is produced by the opposite type of labor.

The link-up entails many necessary functions. For example, they bestow upon the Active Population and Consumer Goods a common characteristic which enables them to interact as quantitatively comparable material. Put another way, the Conduits provide a device for comparing oranges and apples. Two opposite entities are quantitatively comparable with respect to their common characteristic embodied in the form of the Conduit.

Another potent example is the case of capitalist society. There, consumer goods and human energy are clothed with a money medium and are exchanged for money prices and money wages in consumer goods markets and markets for human energy.

Finally, Human Labor requires a natural terminus, together with a corresponding natural start-up of a new cycle. This function is the role of the Accumulation of Wealth in the form of a synthesis of Inertial Matter and Inertial Births.

Human Labor in Action

The Effective Population is the workhorse of the labor engine. It is the subject of both phases of Human Labor. it performs the dual function of "huffing and puffing", of "exhaling and inhaling, of expelling and absorbing. It is the expulsion of the Active Population and the reverse absorption of Consumer Goods by the same Effective Population that initiate the two phases of labor.

To fix ideas, consider the fact that purposeful activities can only be initiated by the conscious will of people. It is this attribute of human beings that causes autonomous behavior directed toward preconceived results. Non-human matter possesses no subconscious will to action.

The Effective Population sends the Active Population in motion to External Labor by way of a Conduit. This act requires the exertion of two types of energy. The energy that binds the Active Population to the Inertial Births must be overcome before the Active Population can be separated from Internal Labor, and therefore from its bedmate Inertial Births, in order to enter External Labor to participate in the reproduction of non-human matter`.

The inward thrust of Active Population against Internal Labor environs starts the process of new births by the Active Population to begin the first phase in the reproduction of the Inertial Births. At the same time, the outward thrust of energy is carried by the Active Population on its way to absorption and death in External Labor. The sum of these two types of energy is exactly the energy provided by the Effective Population to External Labor.

Separating the Active Population from the Inertial Births is to overcome the binding energy that holds it to the Inertial Births in the Internal Labor Process. This is accomplished by reproducing the birth phase of the Inertial Births. The sum of the energy expended to produce the births of the Inertial Births, plus the energy of the Active Population itself, is the total energy carried into External Labor to produce Non-human Matter.

These two equations below illustrate this description.

$$f2[A(T\text{-}100)] = C(T\text{-}100) + K(T\text{-}100).$$

$$I(t) = f1[C(t)] - A(t);\ t = 1, 2, ., (T\text{-}00).$$

The first equation describes the initial conditions for the performing External Labor during the Current Cycle. It depicts the end result of Internal Labor during the Initial Period. It states that the Internal Labor during the Initial Period created Effective Population of an amount of energy equal to the energies of the Consumer Goods and Inertial Matter used up in Internal Labor.

The second equation describes the start of the Current Cycle of External Labor.

It describes the Accumulation of Inertial Births, I(t), where t starts from (T-100) and will run up to T. It is simultaneously creating the birth state of the Inertial Births, while sending the Active Population off on its mission of death to External Labor.

f2[A(t)] is the use of Active Population by the Effective Non-human Matter. This measures the quantity of External Labor created by this activity.

A(t) is Active Population. The negative sign means that it has left the Internal Labor phase, and is passing through the Conduit to its destination in the External Labor phase.

The overall result of these two equations is that the External Labor Process depends on some results of the Internal Labor Process.

The Accumulation of Inertial Births follows the end of the Internal Labor phase. However, it starts the next phase of External Labor by providing the Active Population to the External Labor Process to start its operation.

The two equations below illustrate the description of the Accumulation of Inertial Non-Human Matter.

$$f1[C(t)] = A(T\text{-}100)) + I(T\text{-}100).$$
$$K(t) = f2[A(t)] - C(t);\ t=1,2,..,T(100).$$

The first equation describes the initial conditions for performing Internal Labor during the Current Cycle. It depicts the end result of

External Labor during the Initial Period. It states that the External Labor during the Initial Period created Non-Human Matter of an amount of energy equal to the energies of the Active Population and the Inertial Births used up in External Labor

The second equation describes the start of the Current Cycle of Internal Labor. It describes the Accumulation of Inertial Matter, K(t), where t starts from (T-100) and will run up to T. It is simultaneously creating the active state of Inertial Matter, while sending the Consumer Goods off on its mission of being used up in Internal Labor.

The first equation is the use of Consumer Goods by the Active Population. This measures the quantity of Internal Labor created by this activity.

The negative sign on the Consumer Goods means that it has left the External Labor phase, and is passing through the Conduit to its destination in the Internal Labor phase.

The Accumulation of Inertial Matter follows the end of External Labor. However, it starts the next phase of Internal Labor by providing Consumer Goods to start its operations

The overall result of these two equations is that the Internal Labor Process depends on some results of the External Labor Process.

The Accumulation of Inertial Non-human Matter will end the External Labor Process. However, it is seen that it provides the Consumer Goods to the Internal Labor Process to start and complete its operation.

The role of Human Labor is a crucial phase in population formation. It is the strategic activity that brings the population into reality—creating a special species consisting of discrete individual elements, but possessing attributes more powerful than its individual components, and behaving quite independent of these components.

Moreover, Human Labor is seen to transcend population reproduction alone. It likewise reproduces the population's non-human means of survival. As a matter of fact, it would have been impossible to reproduce the population without this dual responsibility.

But under different rules of engagement in the operation of the core sets of its accompanying institutions Human Labor could very well produce different types of population. That is to say, it may be the source of a typology of population.

The system of population reproduction, based on different sets of rules of engagement, constitutes what we call a Political Economy. It is at once the architectural plan and the engineering construction specs that distinguish one population from another. It guides the population formation task and makes it into an enduring structure.

Political Economies are believed to be subject to a systematic, evolutionary development over time. While there may be different flavors of the same type, nevertheless, a specific type stands, at any given time, inside an historical era. Whatever this stage of development, it has already experienced all previous evolutionary types, and is poised to enter the next developmental stage in the future.

4

Political Economy

POPULATION COMES IN many varieties. Throughout the epochs many types have been created in the imagination of religious and secular writers. Today, a large number of distinctive types are observed throughout the real world. Moreover, close monitoring of the history of any one of these real world populations will reveal that it has undergone a progressive evolution through one or more distinctive types. And its present status is the last phase in a series of evolutionary transformations, from an initial type through other intermediary types, to its current genre.

We are tempted to speculate that an appropriate line-up of all existing real world populations would reflect the underlying general pattern of evolution of population types. At the same time such a line-up would exemplify the differential time-origin and speed of evolution of any given population, compared to any other.

A typology of populations may prove very helpful in comprehending the complex variety and colorful array of distinct populations currently occupying the world stage. The construction of such a typology, however, requires some unifying principle by which the classification may come to closure.

General Population Type

Consider a group of people, who are residing within a well-defined geographic domain, under the jurisdiction of a political state. Assume further that each year, without fail, the members of this group are required to produce two sets of materials—a crop of human babies and a crop of food.

These two sets of rules are (a) Rules of Internal Labor, for production of the baby crop; and (b) Rules of External Labor, for producing the food crop.

Under these circumstances a rule for distributing an annual ration of food among the annual crop of babies is required.

In addition, there must be a rule for distributing members of the population to the tasks involved in food production.

These two sets of rules are (a) Rules of Distribution of food from External Labor, where it is produced, to Internal Labor, where it is used; and (b) Rules of Distribution of people from Internal Labor, where they are produced, to External Labor, where they are used.

These Rules may be thought of as provisions of passageways that enable the food and human agents to transit from the source of their origin to the location of their demise. These dual, but opposite, movements bind the two Labor processes in a continuous cycle of baby and food reproducing operations.

One possible rule for distributing the food is that 100 percent of any given year's food crop is to be reserved for the lifetime use of the corresponding year's baby crop.

Assume further that each baby is allocated an equal quantity of the total annual food supply. Thus, the potential longevity of each baby is determined by the annual per-baby food production, divided by the annual quantity of food biologically required to sustain a baby's life.

Food is a highly perishable material. If it is not consumed rather quickly it decays. Thus, the lifetime allocation of food to each baby needs to be preserved over the years of life of the baby. This can be accomplished if a "social refrigerated warehouse" for storing the food, not currently consumed by the most recent baby crop, is put into service. This rule helps to define some of the details of Internal Labor. It relates the maintenance and longevity of life to the consumption of food.

Assume that all surviving population members serve collectively as such a warehouse, insofar as they are required to consume the total annual food supply. Now sated with the life-giving energies from food consumption, the population members are now able to engage in pair-wise embraces, according to prevailing mores and social strictures, to produce a new baby crop during the ensuing year.

Once the annual food supplies are exhausted through consumption by the population members, they must be renewed during the ensuing year. To create a new supply, a "social allocation rule" is required to distribute members of the population among the tasks involved in food production. This Rule helps to define some of the details of External Labor.

Assume also that members are assigned, according to their skills, to till the soil and perform other activities connected with food production.

Sated with energies from the consumption of food, population members are able to undertake the production tasks. This saps and destroys their energies. But at the same time, they create a new crop of food.

In order to link up the two phases of producing babies and producing food we need a "social passageway" that allows for the movement of food from where it is produced, to where it is used. At the same time that passageway must also allow for the movement of population members from where they are produced to where they are used.

The social passageway is a Conduit, consisting of a material whose composition is a synthesis of babies and food. Such a material has the capability of setting a standard of quantitative comparison between population members and their food supply.

We will designate this standard of quantitative comparison as "Wealth".

Production of the food supply is accomplished by members of the population using up their energies, external to themselves, upon the pristine earth. Production of the baby crop is accomplished by members of the population by using up their energies internally upon themselves.

These two activities of producing babies and producing food, joined together by the wealth material of the pathways, continuously reproduce the people and their material means of survival.

A social "rule of wealth accumulation" sets the stage for the end of one cycle of reproduction and the start of a new cycle of reproduction.

The reproducing process must have a completion. But since it is continuous, it must have a natural re-start capability. End and re-start mechanisms must be organically related. We assume that wealth performs this function.

Wealth is the passageway that connects the two Labor processes; Accumulation of wealth is the process that separates the two opposite phases of Labor. As each performs its role as object of labor, Accumulation plays the role of "ender" of Labor. In the roles of Accumulator, they play the roles of "starters".

Wealth then becomes a natural simultaneous ender and re-starter of the production of population members and their food supply.

This role is a very critical one in the activities of the Political Economy. It possesses the potential for helping to distinguish between different types of Political Economies. The distinction may be based on the specific form of wealth prevailing. Any two types of Political Economies differ if the prevailing type of wealth differ. It is as simple as that.

The type of wealth determines the nature of the link-up of the two processes of production. Hence, it determines the nature of the reproduction processes. The two go hand in hand, and must form a friendly partnership.

Associated with the quantitative change of the Political Economy with the same form of wealth prevailing, over a span of years, is the possibility of a change in the type of wealth at the end of the period of time. A rule of "Accumulation of Wealth" is required to accommodate this condition.

We assume that the function of wealth is two-fold. On the one hand, it is the field in which the agents of production of babies and production of food are enabled to move to the destination of their activity. This is a synthesizing function.

We assume further that Accumulation of Wealth is an analytic function. That is, it brings to an end the operation of the two production activities. It is the separation, the cessation, of action. It is the natural end of the cycle of reproduction of babies and of food.

This hypothetical population harbors a host of possibilities. Foremost among them is that the formulations of the various "rules" as a consistent set of specifications could very well define a political economy and its attendant population type.

A key to the consistency of the rules could be found in the type of wealth. For example, it if is of human form, then we may encounter a slave Political Economy. If it is of land form, then we may encounter a share-cropping Political Economy. If it is of money form, we may encounter a capitalist Political Economy.

Furthermore, the possibility exists that quantitative changes in wealth over long periods of time may induce non-quantitative changes in population reproducing activities. Such changes may also alter the defining characteristic traits of population members who must carry out population activities. Should this occur, wealth could very well take on a different form than heretofore.

This hypothetical population exhibits many of the essential characteristics of a real population. With appropriate modifications, it is possible to make a direct connection between fiction and reality.

Forms of Wealth

The range of possible types of wealth is very limited. Its function is to unite the two phases of Human Labor; at the same time its function is to separate the two phases of labor. It must therefore consist of a material form that has both of these attributes.

We surmise that Inertial Births and Inertial Earth Matter have these capabilities. Inertial Births is the object of Internal Labor; Inertial earth

Matter is the object of External Labor. The changed state of each when involved in its respective labor activity is the conversion to its inertial state, but in a shattered mode. At the same time, the cleanup of its mess, its being put back together, the Accumulation, starts the cycle of labor all over again.

Endings and beginnings are the attributes of wealth.

The rules of wealth formation and accumulation, the rules of distribution of the population to produce the means of survival of the population, the rules of distribution of consumer goods to be used by the population to reproduce itself—all of these rules must be internally consistent to define a specific type of Political Economy.

This discussion of the various roles and characteristics of wealth suggests that wealth is a form of the Gang of 2. It is, indeed, a synthesis of two opposite elements—Inertial Births and Inertial Matter. These two elements are appropriate proxies for human earth matter and non-human earth matter.

It follows that wealth must have a separate existence from either of its elements. However, its form must be the same as (a) one of its elements, or (b) the other element, or (c) both of the elements, or (d) none of the elements.

In its role as conduit, as synthesis, accumulator, it must have the properties of both of its elements. An example is the case of money in a capitalist society. In its consumer goods market and the market for human energy it readily converts into consumer goods or into human energy.

In capitalist society, money also serves as the object of accumulation. In this role, it is neither consumer good nor human, but may well be gold or some other precious metal.

It would seem that slaves are the objects of accumulation while land plays this role in sharecropping societies.

In any event, the distinctive ways in which the Effective Population engages in Human Labor Activity to reproduce itself and to reproduce the non-human means of survival, different types of political economies are generated.

The Political Economy is a Gang of 2 genre, standing near the top of the hierarchy of population formation. At the bottom is the single human life, born of adult parents, in a family arena, encased in a Quantum Cocoon of annual births, and slotted in a reserved location in a time frame. This phenomenon is then aggregated into groups of births called Active Population and Inertial Births, which engage in the activity of Human Labor under the rules of operation of a Political Economy.

The hierarchical journey represents social and other constraints that serve as limits to the actions of the individuals who stand at the bottom of the hierarchy. To be sure, such individuals behave with confidence that they are free and independent and can effectively exercise choice in their everyday lives. The constraints are ignored because they synchronize so well with human life that they function like genetic imperatives, hard-wired into each individual's biological structures.

But the Political Economy stage is not the end of the line. It is suffused with rules of engagement. Hence, there is a need for an ordered existence of the population in the Political Economy.

Indeed, it is the role of the Political Sate to promulgate the rules, to monitor these rules, and to enforce these rules in order that the Political State may function to preserve the lives of its inhabitants.

5

Political State

THE POLITICAL STATE is the most powerful institution in the web of constraints on the activities of the population member. It tolerates no competitor in wielding its power. It is the sole unbridled manager of the conduct of the Political Economy

> It promulgates the rules of operation of the Political Economy. It monitors and enforces those rules with an iron fist. It garners unto itself a monopoly of force and violence that ensures its supreme power over any would be foreign or domestic rebel against its edicts.

Each type of Political Economy has its own peculiar set of rules. These rules originate out of the evolutionary development of Political Economies. The critical factor in the evolutionary process is the form in which wealth occurs. Intimately associated with the form of wealth is the nature of the relations among classes of population members based on ownership of wealth.

In a general way wealth evolves from a type that is associated with no private property to types with private property generating different classes of people.

Primitive communal society is a type in which the Political Economy is based on common ownership of the land on which the food and other goods are produced, common ownership of the food and other means of survival, common rearing of the children. This type of society is associated with hunters and gatherers, and fishers. It is dominated by food production and food consumption. Very little else takes place.

A second stage in the evolutionary process occurs with both the pristine land and the people who work the land are the private property of a class of slave owners. The material form of wealth is the slave.

> A third stage in the evolutionary process is one in which the land is still the private property of landlords; the landless people are the working class who have some measure of ownership of themselves, but are tied to working the land for life by some sort of formal agreement with the landowners. For the working class, very little beyond food is made available for consumption.
>
> A fourth stage in the evolutionary process is one in which one class of people privately own wealth in the form of money; the working class owns private property in themselves, but they must obtain the means of survival and acquire the right to labor if they are successful in receiving employment by means of market relations with the wealth owners.

Other types of mythical societies have been created in the imaginations of religious and secular writers. One interesting one has to do with two adults living in the largesse of a garden of ease and comfort, in which no labor is required to provide the food necessary for their survival.

Unfortunately, these two adults soon embraced and created a seed which began to gestate in the body of the female. This was a signal to evict them from the garden to live in exile on earth. Here they continued to enjoy the free field of air from which they could exhale and inhale to help in the maintenance of life. However, they were now impelled to produce the food for themselves and for any upcoming offspring.

Post-money societies have also been imagined--El Dorado, Utopia, People's Democracy, Socialist, Communist. Close scrutiny of these types has shown them to be at best "pseudo" transition types. In the main, the Chinese and Russian examples of Socialism or Communism have turned out to be attempts by the USSR and by the Chinese Communist Party to use their power to speed up the development of the money based Political Economy.

An example of the power and sway of the Political State over the activities of the individual population member is the case of the United States. The complex interactions between all the levels of government boggles the imagination.

The individual is subject to the rules and regulations of local government units, standing in a hierarchical organization. These may involve water districts, zoning districts, towns, areas of towns outside of villages, villages, cities, counties.

Above these units are state government and its coterie of supporting agencies, which form another set of government enforcers in the hierarchy of management of the Political Economy. They may also be involved in interstate compacts, like the Port Authority of New York, Connecticut, and New Jersey

Still above these units are the arms of the federal government with its overarching controls. This unit may also be responsible for administering international treaties and other obligations in conjunction with the United Nations.

In summary, the Political State's management function is to preserve the integrity of the Political Economy. It creates an organization, a bureaucracy, to carry out its mission to administer the rules it promulgates. Much of the administration turns on protecting the private property rights of the members of the society. This responsibility is the key to the temporal continuity of the Political Economy.

But in consort with the concept of evolution, the quantitative development of a given Political Economy gives way at some point in time to forces which engender qualitative disruption, and a new type of Political Economy is born.

We have come a long way from the birth of a new population member, from the activities of two adult parents, within a family arena, encased in a quantum cocoon, in a unique slot in a time-frame. And all these states of affairs of this one new born infant was seen to be subject to a series of potent constraints of aggregated births formed into strategic groups, poised at the ready to perform Human Labor.

We saw the further constraints of Labor, operating in two phases, to reproduce not only the population as a functioning engine, but also to reproduce the means of survival of that population.

But the enhanced role of Labor required some measure of control to preserve the integrity of the system of Political Economy which it created. The Political State does not operate in a vacuum. It is grounded in the earth, in an environment of many different types of Political States which impacts its operation.

At the same time, the earthly domain provides the material substrata out of which both the human population and its non-human means of survival are ultimately created.

The earth environment in which the source of population membership comes to life is the last great constraint on this novel creation of humanity. It is the source of the material substratum of both the human population and its means of survival.

The range of earth materials available to a political state sets limits to the opportunities of a political state to execute Human Labor. A political state located in the Sahara Desert may be less able to provide its people with a variety of goods and services, compared to a political state located in the northern temperate zone.

The state of bilateral political relations between states may play a big role in the opportunities of a political state. Wars of conquest of one large state by another smaller or weaker state is a highly probable circumstance. Exploitation of a smaller state by a more powerful foe by way of economic exploitation is also highly possible.

The worldly arena in which a political state finds itself is therefore a very important source of constraints on individual behavior in population activities.

6

Impact of Earth Space

PERHAPS THE MOST telling constraint on the individual population member is the earth space in which it comes to life.

The earth is the source material of which the population member as well as its survival goods are composed. Human earth matter and non-human earth matter are the two opposing elements that are synthesized to make the new born babies and their food supply. The act of Human Labor is indeed the transformation of non-human earth matter into human earth matter; and the transformation of earth matter into non-human earth matter.

The earth is also standing ground upon which Human Labor functions. It is the solid foundation upon which all population formation activities are embedded by the force of gravity or whatever it is that holds them plantwise bound to their earthly abode, keeping them from straying far away into the cosmos.

The earth is also the opportunity factor for the creation of specific survival materials of the population. The attributes of the soil which make possible the production of specific types of fruit and vegetables; the forests that provide lumber for the building of housing abodes and non-human production facilities; the existence of rivers and lakes and oceans that provide the largesse of fish and other seafood and enable the construction of transportation networks that connect ports along the way—these and more attributes of the earth set the limits on the dimensions of population reproducing activities.

Finally, the earth is the operating arena of all the various types of Political States with which any one Political State must interact. A colorful panorama of Political States of all types in the evolutionary scheme exert their impacts. This is a crucial point in the sense that the earth environment is the general arena of outside influences that may have differential effects on the outcomes of Political States during the same time period as well as in different time periods.

In the period following on World War I, the powerful capitalist Political States of Europe imposed their will upon the non-capitalist states of Africa, conquered them and ruled them as subject colonies. This is one telling example of how "outside" world can affect an "inside" Political State.

Another interesting example is the wars of conquest and enslavement of many peoples throughout the African continent during the 15th to the 19th centuries. Primitive communal, slave, feudal African states fell to the superior armed might of the European marauders and wrought havoc on the African people that is still being felt in the early part of the 21st century.

We should now have a picture of a population, from the birth of its individual member, through many time and social constraints, subject to the rules of the Political State, which itself is impacted by the worldwide environment in which it operates.

Among the world environment is the existence of individuals in outside populations who depart from their population of their birth and migrate to other populations. Under certain circumstances these migrants affect population outcomes in many important ways. However, their contribution to host population outcomes can be understood by conceiving of the entering migrants as an auxiliary source of new membership.

Migrant entry can be likened to births; migrant years of residence in the host population domain can be likened to age of the births during the Current Year of entry. Using this analogous conception, all the results obtained for births can then be applied to the migrant process.

In the following chapter we pursue a discussion of the role of Migration in population growth and development. This is a telling example of the earth environment on population formation and growth.

7

Migration as a Source of Population Membership

In Chapter 1 we defined a human population as a closed group under the binary activity of birthing-- a specialized process in which two adult members of the population unite to generate a new baby, which is itself also a member of the population. In a world in which many different populations exist, and to the extent that there is effective opportunity for contact between distinct populations, the possibility exists that persons will move, with varying degrees of freedom, between the geographic domains of the various populations. It is therefore necessary to consider how the interchange of individuals between different geographic domains affect population membership.

The proximate reasons for migration reside within the conscious will of the individual migrant. But whatever impels a person to migrate, the actual move is constrained by a number of circumstances beyond the control of the potential migrant. These constraints consist of a complex set of opportunity factors that are effectively available for making the migratory move. Such factors may exist within the geographic domain of the potential migrant, or that of the population toward which the move is contemplated, or in the intersecting relations among all the different world populations.

Legal restrictions on migration may be relevant. Other factors may involve the nature of economic development, the political infrastructure, the state of religious and other freedoms, the nature of the cultural milieu, the extent of wars among nations, the degree of international political détente, and a host of unforeseen circumstances. But whatever impels a specific individual to migrate, that one person's entry into the domain of a population from an alien domain has negligible impact on the host population membership. Indeed, it is the migration of a significantly large number of individuals over a sustained period of time that generates change in the receiving population membership.

Migrant impact on population membership therefore depends upon a systematic operation of one or more factors that impel migrations on a large and continuing scale in the domain of the receiving population or in the domains of one or more alien populations. Drought in agricultural lands and its accompanying famine may be such an event. Economic depression and its accompanying large scale unemployment in the sending domain may be another such factor. Still another factor may be economic expansion in the host domain. The degree to which these events occur and the extent of receptivity on the part of the receiving population will provide potential impacts on population membership.

Any individual who moves between the geographic domains of two distinctive populations will be referred to as a "migrant". We distinguish different types of migrants. "Migrants" are the inputs of individuals from an alien population to a host population. Once inside the host population, migrants become separated into two groups--"Immigrants", who are the subset of "living" migrants; and "Inertial Migrants", who are dead migrants.

Input of Migrants

The conceptual notion of migration is derived from the operation of three distinct, but interrelated, processes. First, there is the "input of migrants" from abroad into the domestic geographic domain. Second, there is the conversion of Migrants into "Immigrants" and "Inertial Migrants "inside the domestic geographic domain. Third, there is the "Accumulation of Inertial Migrants"; that is, the transformation of Migrants into population members.

The input of Immigrants manifests itself as a number of persons who have departed various countries for a final entry to the host population. These people come with a baggage of characteristics which they inherited from birth, and which they acquired as a consequence of being historically molded by their original native population upbringing. They speak a language which may or may not be the language of the host population. They may be adherents of one or more religious orders. They possess a specific distribution of age, education, formal schooling, private economic resources, and a bevy of other attributes. Therefore, at the time of entry to the U.S. they are not population members. One of their important traits is the fact that they were not born of host population parentage. At the time of entry they are not yet *bona fide* members of the host population.

The events we have presented thus far in this chapter describe the first phase in the migration process—the input of Migrants from abroad. In some real cases, the number of entering migrants over the course of a cycle can run into the millions.

Conversion of Migrants

Acquisition of the status of Immigrants and Inertial Migrants is the process of distribution of the components of the Migrants of the past years among the domestic population members during the Current Year. This involves their integration into the domestic population as direct participants in population reproducing activities in a coordinated way with the existing members of the domestic population. Distribution of the Migrants by age is apparently the decisive process. However, for analytic purposes, we shall choose two criteria—the year of entry, and the residential age during the Current Year of entry. The number of years of residence in the host population constitutes the most practical index for age of migrants. A Migrant, therefore, is an entrant to the host population who may be alive or dead, and who, during the current year, has been resident in the host for a specific number of years.

We should note in passing that years of residence ("RA") runs the gamut serially from zero to ninety-nine. Hence, the distribution of Migrants among the hundred RA's during the current year precisely reflects the serial entry of the surviving residue of Migrants over the previous ninety-nine years and the Current Year. In any given Current Year, therefore, this conception pinpoints the location of each Migrant in a population age-group that is precisely equal to its RA.

It is obvious that this distribution of Migrants provides a natural basis for their integration into the domestic population and thus enables them to participate in population reproducing activities. As such, they will be subject to the same forces of wear and tear and ultimate decay as the domestic population members.

Accumulation of Migrants

Finally, as a consequence of direct participation in population reproducing activities, the Migrants will experience the wear and tear of their labors and some will succumb to death, and of course, some will survive. The process doesn't end here, however. The dead Migrants must be reproduced as dead potential population members and the Immigrants must be reproduced as living potential population members. In both cases the reproduced entities must be born of (a) population members, (b) migrants, (c) mixtures of population members and migrants.

We have no way of determining which of these possibilities will hold. Nevertheless, we think it is of no great moment. The practical outcome is that in the actual count of population members, as done with a census, the Immigrants will be represented. And since the way in which we have integrated the Migrants into the population by way of their ID within the time frame, their numbers will appear as an auxiliary birth event. Migrant contribution to the quantitative attribute of the population will be similar to what is contributed by such an auxiliary birthing machine.

The essential role of Migrants in population formation is that of a "primitive" source of population formation. The source is primitive in the sense that it originated outside the domestic population, but is destined to become in time a necessary part of the domestic population. In short, the Migrants will take their places among their domestic cohorts and will participate in all domestic population activities. They will die within the domestic population; but they (as well as other domestic population members) will give birth to replace the deaths. Thus, in time, their numerical impact on the domestic population will derive from the fact that they will first die within the domestic geographic domain, and then, subsequently will be replaced by domestic births.

It is precisely this process of reproduction of the Migrants which determines their lasting impact on the quantity and attributes of the domestic population membership. The reproduction may take any of three possibilities—negative, or neutral, or positive. If the positive case prevails, then the Migrants will exert an increasing impact on population membership with its attendant increasing influence on the attributes of the population. It would thus appear that the "Velocity of Migration" is the relevant parameter for measuring the lasting impact of Migrant entry and the consequent results on Migrant reproduction.

> It is this new addition to the birthing scheme within the domestic population that creates the force for a change in the birthing pattern. Thus, a possibility for an increase in the number of births over and beyond the simple reproduction level becomes a reality.

Summary

In sum, once the Migrants have entered the host population, they take up residential status in the geographic domain as quasi-members of the population. During the Current Year, all those Migrants in residential age groups (99-199) will be definitely dead; those in RA between (0-99) will contain some dead and some living members. We shall hereafter refer to the Migrants in this latter RA as "Effective Migrants". Thus, the "velocity of Effective Migrants" is the relevant parameter for measuring the impact of Migration.

8

Effective Population

THE EFFECTIVE POPULATION is the heart of population activity. It is a synthesis of the past and future generations. It serves as the sink of the previous cycles of population formation; simultaneously, it serves as the fount of the future cycle of population formation.

It accomplishes this remarkable feat by cloning the initial Effective Population; at the same time, it appends an increment to the cloned population. The increment may be positive, negative, or zero. But whatever it is, it points to a well-defined path to the future Effective Population.

We may therefore conclude that it is the Current Cycle serving as the present generations of population reproduction activities. It is likewise the past generations, encompassing within its structure all the previous cycles of population formation. Finally, it is the future, inasmuch as it will become an integral base for the future Cycle of population formation.

Past, present, future—all wrapped into one Effective Population. This is the magic of this dynamic segment of the total population.

Individual Births

Every population member is the repository of a set of non-quantitative traits. Any analysis of population membership is therefore inadequate without a specification of these attributes, or at least a mention of the most significant ones.

Such traits are important precisely because the unique conscious will of each member exercises these traits whenever it is engaged in population reproduction activities. To be sure, the application of the conscious will is circumscribed by a web of intertwined historical, social, and biological circumstances into which the member is born and grows and develops.

Of major importance among these circumstances is the constraint of time. At birth the population member is encased within an annual Quantum Cocoon, consisting of all the births that took place during the year of birth. The cocoon is identified with the year of birth and the age during the Current Year.

The individual member's activities can be easily traced inside the web of circumstances connected with the exercise of conscious will inside the complex of constraints on unique individual behavior.

The cooperative exercise of individual traits by all or by strategic groups of individuals transforms these traits into population actions. The specific form and outcome of the population actions are quite immune from the impact of any one individual's behavior.

A population is made up of many single individuals who originate out of a birthing activity. These were discussed at length in Chapter 2.

Every one of these individuals is a repository of a vector of human attributes. Among the elements of the vector are two identifiers—year of birth and age during the Current Year.

Within the Effective Population every individual can be identified with an age group, from zero to 99. Depending upon the Political State of which the population is a part, much of the individual activities are done by age groupings.

A few categories help to classify the types of activities that are heavily dependent upon age.

First, and quite important, is the category of the new born, the babies. They own the zero-age group. These are the youngest of all age groups. They are born during the Current Year. An important attribute of this group is that it is has a specific year of birth which is also the population's year of birth. Their importance, of course, is that they are the source of population origin, and of population continuity.

Children are of ages between 0 and the age at which it is biologically possible to give birth These individuals are generally dependent on their parents or other guardians for maintaining their lives.

Adults occupy the ages from childhood to potential longevity. This is the group which actively participates in birthing and which provides the main avenue of support for the Children.

Older members of this group who no longer actively participate in birthing are the Elders.

More formally, the Effective Population consists of two major age groupings—Children and Adults. This hierarchy mirrors the dependency and support mechanism of population activity. As we go up the hierarchy we encounter the growth in the degree of independent action by population members. Independent activities are more circumscribed the younger the individual. A more age-regimented set of activities dominate. At the adult level activity becomes more diverse and appear to be exceedingly random in time and content.

The age distribution also implies a time period during which members must be kept alive. In particular, the activities which accomplish this task involve feeding, housing, clothing, moralizing, politicizing, developing specific work skills, and a host of other functions.

These activities depend upon the personal consumption of food and other materials by each individual member of the population. But the continuity of such activities likewise requires a set of related activities by which the member engages in the creation of food and other materials which are consumed personally by the members.

Individual activities require the application of the conscious will of each individual. This is possible to the extent that such individual is alive. In particular, a birthing activity requires at least two living adults, one of whom is male and the other female. Thus, a distribution of population members by mortality and by gender are implied.

Gender Distribution

The distribution of gender among the members of the Effective Population is a binomial distribution. The exact knowledge of the probability of a male or female is not of critical moment. The very existence of the Effective Population presupposes the existence of a viable division of the adults among the two genders. The protracted existence of the Effective Population over a long span of years likewise presupposes some stability in the distribution.

In any event, birthing implies the existence of adequate opportunities for pairs of adults to meet, to court, to consciously surrender their wills in mutual agreement to participate in family formation and birthing activities. Such opportunities reside in the frequency and intensity of mutual contacts, conditioned by mores and folkways, ethnic origin, religion, education, local customs, language, age-bound capabilities, and a host of other social restrictions on individual behavior.

Mortality Status

Mortality status of members of the Effective Population is subject to some very simple principles.

Actual deaths of individuals come after they are born. Year of birth and age during the Current Year are two opposite states of an individual's life. After all, year of birth is the start of life of that individual; age during the Current Year is the end of life to date of that same individual.

When births are aggregated to form Effective Population groups, the aggregate years of birth of individuals become years of survival; the corresponding aggregate of age during the Current Year is years of death. These two opposite attributes are the corresponding aggregate years of birth for the period of aggregation within the Effective Population.

Within the Effective Population, death comes in two varieties. The Inertial Births are reproduced by first getting born and subsequently dying. Birth and death occur in that order within the Current Cycle. Of critical importance is the fact that the death-state of Inertial Births occur strictly within the Internal Labor process as a consequence of its role as object of External Labor.

During this same Cycle the Active Population of the Initial Cycle first dies and subsequently born. Death and birth occur in that order within the Current Cycle. Unlike the Inertial Births, the Active Population dies inside the External Labor Process as a consequence of its role in producing the food and other non-human means of survival. Of course, it is born within the Internal Labor Process as a consequence of the transformation of food and other consumer goods into human energy.

The reproduction of the Inertial Births is the stabilizing attribute of the Effective Population. It is in synchrony with the individual potentiality to survive somewhere between zero and 100 years.

The reproduction of the Active Population, on the other hand, is the potential for continuity into the future. Its death calls forth its birth. It was born in a previous cycle. It transcended the previous cycle to continue its life in the Current Cycle. It dies and then gets born in the Current Cycle.

There is more to the story of the Active Population. Since it is the living segment of the Initial Population, it must be the engine that generates all the births during the Current Cycle. It must produce enough births during the Current Cycle to equal (a) its initial state, (b) its growth, (c) the initial Inertial Births, (d) growth of the Initial Inertial Births.

This leads us to a powerful result of birthing. The Active Population during the Current Year is a function of the aggregate of all individual years of birth from the first year of the Total Population formation to the Current Year. The astute reader should recognize that our hypothetical Active Population is the phenomenon generally referred to as the Census of Population.

These observations identify the specific components of the mortality configuration of the Effective Population. Yet, mere identification does not indicate the essential role of death. Death is the dead weight of the population. Such concepts as inertia, mass, etc. help to visualize the substance of this role.

Organic Composition

For the individual member, death comes about from a number of causes. For the population, however, death is the wear and tear on the collective body as a consequence of the expenditure of energy in the production of food and other non-Human materials necessary to maintain the lives of the population members.

Inertial Births get their comeuppance when playing the role of object of External Labor. The energy impelled into it by the Consumer Goods, in their entry to the Internal Labor process, wreaks death upon the Inertial Births.

Active Population meets its demise during its transformation into Non-human goods inside the External Labor Process.

Such collective wear and tear manifest themselves currently in the demise of a number of members, who are distributed throughout all age groups in the Effective Population.

Birth and the maintenance of life result from the activity of consuming the food and other non-human goods. This activity replenishes the energies of the members of all ages throughout the Effective Population. The result during the Current Year is the total surviving members of the Effective Population.

Strategic Grouping of Births

The source of population activity is manifested in the collective action of population members from the year of origin of the population up through the Current Year. Thus, the temporal pattern of birth is the significant parameter determining the position of a member in the structure of the population.

Every member of the population is identified with its specific year of birth and its age during the Current Year. If we designate the age during the Current Year as "Implicit Age", then the population membership is naturally structured as a number of Implicit Age groups, ranging downward in integer units from zero to the Current Year minus 1. These same groups can be identified with the related "year of birth", ranging upward in integer units from 1 to the Current Year.

Various combinations of such groups are associated with strategic operational segments of the population. For starters, let us identify the group with Implicit Age equal to or greater than 100. This group is what we call the Past Generations.

Every member of this group was born prior to the Current Year minus 99. During the Current Year, they are all dead. Each has completed its potential longevity. Later in this chapter we will describe the important function that this group plays.

A second group consists of all population member with Implicit Age less than zero. This group is the "Future Generations". No member of this group has yet been born. These are only potential members of the population.

A third, and most important group, consists of all members with Implicit Age from zero to 99. This group is the Effective Population, and is the subject matter of this chapter. It is the "Present Generations".

This group was born during the period from the Current Year Minus 99, to the Current Year. It is therefore confined to a period enclosing the Current Cycle of population formation

The mortality structure of this group is a combination of members, some of whom are alive and some of whom are dead. Observation of any real world population will only yield up the surviving segment; the dead ones will not be visible to the observer. However, we will demonstrate in the sequel that each of the survivors carries a mark of death, from which we can easily calculate the corresponding number of dead members in any strategic population group.

These three groups together yield the Total Population—Initial Population and Effective Population. Of interest, we have also indicated the Future Population.

Let us now consider the strategic groups of births which participate in the acts of Human Labor to create the population.

The critical position from which we will view the process of formation of these groups is the view from the perspective of the Current Year, which is the last year of the Current Cycle, consisting of one hundred ordered equal annual years from Current Year Minus 99, to the Current Year.

The Current Cycle is also mated to a downward ordered set of "age during the Current Year", ranging from zero to 99. To fix ideas, the boundaries of the Current Cycle is the coordinates [(T-99),99] to (T,0).

At the beginning of the Current Cycle the population is faced with some critical initial conditions. These conditions consist of the Initial Population, which is the final result of all population activities which ended just prior to the beginning of the Current Cycle. The coordinates which enclose the Initial Population are [1,(T-100)] to [(T-1),100].

Two important population groups make up these initial conditions—Initial Active Population and Initial Inertial Births. The former is the group of survivors and the latter is the group of dead population members.

The two groups define the mortality structure of the Initial Population. They also indicate the strategic role they played in creating the Initial Population.

See Table 2.2 used earlier in chapter 2.

The Initial Active Population is an aggregate of ordered quanta of births which survived from births prior to the Current Cycle. They were therefore part of the result of Internal Labor during the Initial Period. They will serve as instruments of External Labor during the Current Cycle.

The Initial Inertial Births are an aggregate of ordered quanta of births which did not survive from births prior to the Current Cycle. They were therefore part of the results of Internal Labor during the Initial Period. During the Current Cycle, they will serve as Conduits of Consumer Goods from External Labor to Internal Labor. They will also serve as Object of External Labor. Finally, they are destined to play an essential role in the start-up of the Current Cycle.

The Initial Population is the set of initial conditions facing the start of the Current Cycle, whose role is to reproduce the Initial Population.

The strategy for accomplishing this task is two-fold—replace the quantitative attributes of the Initial Population and create an increment thereto. This calls for creation of new births which will reproduce the Initial Active Population as Current Active Population; and reproduce the Initial Inertial Births as Current Inertial Births.

Inertial Births must be born before they die. Both events of birth and death must take place during the Current Cycle. But there is a dilemma; how can dead population members create births. No doubt, they can't. However, they can play an essential role in this endeavor. Let us elaborate.

The process of External Labor is an activity in which the subject is Effective Population, the instrument is Active Population, the Conduit as well as the Object is Inertial Non-Human Matter. The result is the reproduction of Non-Human Matter.

To accomplish this task the Active Population must escape the grasp of the Inertial Births that holds it fast to the Internal Labor System. Only then can it go on its way to enter into External Labor.

The Active Population accomplishes this task by expending a quantity of energy sufficient to overcome the dead weight of the Inertial Births by creating a number of births to counter-balance the dead weight of Internal Births, thereby reproducing the birth-state of Inertial Births.

Recall that births of individuals precede death of individuals. This means that the Active Population carries two sets of energies into External Labor—the energy equivalent of the Inertial Births and its own inherent energy. We speculate that these two sets are the energy carried by the Active Population to reproduce the Non-human goods in the External Labor Process.

At the same time that the Initial Inertial Births are being reproduced as Current Inertial Births, the Initial Active Population is also undergoing its reproduction as Current Active Population.

Recall that it must first die and then reborn to accomplish the reproduction task.

While exercising its energy inside the External Labor to produce Non-human goods, it is undergoing its death march. At the same time, however, the Effective Population is absorbing, ingesting, puffing consumer goods and transforming them into human energy within the Internal Labor Process.

This activity of Internal Labor involves the Consumer Goods as the instrument, Inertial Labor as both Conduit and Object. The Consumer goods are wrenched away from the grip of the Inertial Non-Human goods in the External Labor, sending them into the Inertial Births inside Internal Labor, to be transformed into human energy and consequently into the carriers of that energy—reproduced Inertial Births and reproduced Active Population.

Table 8.1 describes these events.

Population Dynamic

The Effective Population is the work-horse of the Total Population. It is its heart. It beats in obedient response to the constant rhythmic tempo of time, in tandem with the systematic carrying out of the essential activities by its collective membership.

As the Current Year goes out of existence and is succeeded by a new Current Year, the oldest Quantum Coccon of the Elderly Adults quits the environs of the Effective Population and takes its place among the past generations. Simultaneously, the second oldest quantum cocoon of the Elderly move down to occupy the oldest position in the Effective Population.

At the same time the oldest children shed their childhood integuments to become adults. And a group of future members takes its place in the role of a brand new crop of babies.

The result is that part of the Effective Population becomes an integral part of the past generations; part of the future generations joins the fold of the Effective Population; and the internal composition of the Effective Population undergoes an annual change in mortality as well as change in the distribution of member' traits—all in precision stepping to the unvarying tempo of time.

If now we consider a change in the interval of time equal to one cycle, rather than one year, the entire Effective Population will move on to occupy a position among the past generations. Its former place will be occupied by a brand new Effective Population whose membership originated out of the future generations. The dynamical result is that the future generations come to life to replace the present generations; the present generations disappear into the past generations. The accomplishment of all this has been made possible by the birthing activities and by the life-destroying activities, in conjunction with all the other essential population reproducing activities over the specified time interval.

It is as if the entire population undergoes a pulsating internal metamorphosis. At the core is the Effective Population, churning with the activities of its individual members in a frenzy of random intersecting motions.

The phase of contraction is the movement of Active Population and Consumer Goods through their respective Conduits to bond the External Labor and the Internal Labor together, forming a unified system of Human Labor. Here, it makes possible the reproduction of the population and its means of survival.

The phase of expansion is the actual execution of the two phases of labor. It brings into being a new batch of births and a corresponding new batch of the non-human means of survival of the population.

Finally, the balancing of the dynamic tension between the phase of contraction and expansion symbolize the resultant creation of a new Effective Population.

Nothing in the preceding events precludes their repetition over the next succeeding cycle; nor over the cycle following the latter and so on over a long succession of cycles.

The point is that the underlying temporal pattern of births and the inherent temporal pattern of death which drives the former, play the decisive roles in dictating the membership and characteristic signature of the Effective Population throughout exceedingly long periods of time.

The current Effective Population originates out of the past; the same forces which created it will generate the future Effective Population out of the present.

Table 8.1

Human Population Time - Framework

t	I. Initial Population		r
1 ↓ T-100	A. Active Population	B. Inertial Births	T-1 ↑ 100

II. Effective Population

	A. Cloned Initial Population		
1 ↓ T-100	A. Active Population	B. Inertial Births	T-1 ↑ 100

B. Increment Initial Population

T-99 ↓ T	1. Increment to Active Population	2. Increment to Inertial Births	99 ↑ 0

	III. Total Population	
1 ↓ T	I. Initial Population II. Effective Population	T-1 ↑ 0

Legend:

Individual
T - Current Year
t - Year of birth
r - age during
Current Year

Population
Sum of T - Years of Birth
Sum of t - Years of Survival
Sum of r - Years of Death

9

Interfacing the Hypothesis to the Real World

THE PRECEDING CHAPTERS of Part I constitute an interrelated set of hypotheses designed as a description of the real world populations. The task at hand is strictly "description" as opposed to "explanation". We must first know what it is that we are trying to explain. The description should set it apart from everything else as an uniquely identifiable entity. Too many works of scholarship violate this dictum.

The description must be held out as a hypothetical conjecture. Once completed, the hypothetical phenomenon must then be subjected to empirical testing. It must confront reality with the intent of disproving its validity.

If, after very stringent testing the hypothetical entity is not disproved, then we may increase our confidence in its truthful efficacy. This does not mean that we have proved it to be a correct copy of reality; we have only increased our belief that it is a good replica of reality.

More and more future testing is called for as new facts and improved analyses are uncovered.

Existence Postulates

In this work, we have postulated the existence of certain kinds of persons, institutions, operations, and some very specific modes of interplay among them. We have also postulated some special characteristics of time and other instruments of activity which should also be subject to scrutiny. Finally, we have made some critical assumptions about the nature of motion.

All of these presumptions of reality need to be tested against the conditions of the real world before we can even begin to pronounce judgment about the verity of our description of population formation.

We have made use of a conception of motion throughout the work which we can summarize as the "Gang of 2". Others have referred to it as the concept called the "unity of opposites".

A simple statement of this principle is that the dynamic tension between the two opposite elements of the synthesis drives it into motion. Two examples quickly come to mind.

The birthing operation involves two parents of opposite genders—male and female. The synthesis is the creation of a child, who has a separate existence which is independent of that of either parent. The child embodies a new discrete human life.

The creation of the child represents an example of motion. Something new has emerged into the real world. It can then be grouped with all such births during the same year and mated with a specific position on a time scale. Such a position should be uniquely distinguishable from any other birth year grouping.

So soon as other birthings take place the original child's birth group becomes the repository of a lower unit on the time scale; it has acquired an additional year of age. It has also achieved an additional year of survival, an upward move matching the year of ageing.

If we assume that births come in annual quanta, our child is now entangled in an annual Quantum Cocoon of births, containing a certain number of discrete human cohorts. If we associate the quantum with a unique position on the time scale, we can denote that quantum as bT, where b is a constant and T is the Current Year of birth.

If we know the nature of the time scale it is now possible to characterize all annual birth groupings as time-dependent entities.

We postulate that the time scale is a fixed dimension of earth material. It joins with length, width, and height to define the spatial composition of any earth material. Time is conceived to be continuous, capable of being calibrated in equal units, with each unit associated with a moving object.

To keep annual births together in their adventure of motion, we postulate the existence of a Quantum Cocoon into which all births during a given year are encased. During the Current Year, therefore, the quantum cocoon contains a specific number, bT, of discrete human beings. Previous years have their own year of birth time marker, t. These markers are always less than the Current Year, T.

Over a number of years of birthing we can now describe the birthing pattern by the ordered upward sorting of t, from 1 to T.

But every year of birth has its matching counterpart of "age during the Current Year". This number is identically equal to Current Year Minus specific year of birth. The arithmetic is (T-t) identically equal to r.

We now have time slots into which we can imbed every unique Quantum Cocoon. They are T(t,r), for every unique pair, (t,r).

This is a very powerful set of postulates. The pair, (t,r), when summed, gives us the value of the Current Year, T. In short, T is identically equal to t+r.

The Current Year is the synthesis of its two opposite elements, specific year of birth of a population member and the age of that member during the Current Year. We interpret the Current Year as the year of life, the specific year of birth as the start of life, and the age as the end of life to date.

If now we sum each of the three elements, the interpretation takes on a very interesting meaning. The sum of Current Year of birth (ΣT) becomes Aggregate years of Birth; the sum of specific year of births (Σt) becomes Aggregate years of Survival; the sum of age (Σr) becomes Aggregate years of Death.

Finally, during the Current Year, the annual increment in any of the three aggregate measures, each multiplied by the constant, b, is the velocity of the Aggregate. The Velocity of Birth for the population, Velocity of Survival, and Velocity of Death is bT, bt, and br, respectively.

This recitation of postulates and assumptions and the conclusions they generate show the importance of explicit statement of the presumptions about how the real world population is put together.

There is yet a slew of postulates and assumptions in addition to these few which need to be tested in our quest for knowledge of populations.

For example, we have encased each annual crop of births in a quantum cocoon. Each quantum contains a number of discrete births equal in number to the number of families who gave births to the cohorts of that quantum. Each of these families, in turn, is made up of parents and children, every one of which is a member of its own quantum. In short, every member of a family is a member of its own quantum; the families of any given quantum are themselves members of their own quanta and so on, and on, and on.

> Furthermore, we have postulated the aggregated births as forming strategic groupings to play critical roles in the creation of Human Labor, which involves a series of interacting activities by groups of population members, in conjunction with the reproduction of the non-human survival materials of the population.
>
> But this is not all. Human Labor comes in many editions; each type is subject to a specific set of consistent rules of operation. Each of these sets of rules incorporate regulations that include both the reproduction of the population and its non-human means of survival. This is the bailiwick of the Political Economy.

The Political Economy is operated by groups of population members of varying sizes, complexity, classes based on private property ownership. These groups must be managed. Rules must be explicitly promulgated, monitored, and enforced. The most powerful institution in the society, the Political State, usurps this authority.

Finally, the population subsists in a world of Political States, of varying sizes and power, occupying all possible geographic domains. The impact of the Earth on any given Political State also include the standing ground on which the population functions. It also includes the opportunity to create the types of non-human means of survival.

Nature of Empirical Testing

> The observations on the postulates and related assumptions involved in our hypothetical description of a population require some direction in the application of testing against real world events.

We argue that the testing should include the use of the hypothetical population to perform a specific set of activities to produce a definitive result. A command will then be sent to the real world population to perform the same activity. The two results will then be compared to determine their congruity or lack thereof.

Our study was based on an analysis of the U.S. population during the period 1790 to 2000. Our testing of the hypothetical material in Chapters 1-8 will therefore be confined to the United States during the same period.

One extremely important test will concern the creation of the Active Population. This concept is the twin of what is generally called the Census of Population. In fact, layman and scholar alike, generally refer to this phenomenon as "the population".

As you have now seen, we have made "births" to be the essential basis of population. Survivors and dead population members are essential components of the population. Our hypothesis has detailed the critical role played by Inertial Births, dead population members. In any event, we will include the estimate of dead members from a knowledge of the Active Population.

Let the confrontation begin.

Part II
Test of Hypothesis With U.S. Experience

10

The Context of U. S. Populaton Activity

Origins

THE FIRST AND foremost assumption about any population is the existence of a group of people occupying a definable space on the face of the earth during a specified period of time. The group cannot be a simple collection of individuals; indeed, it must be a cohesive social entity, consisting of individuals who have been continuously reproducing themselves among themselves, to the exclusion of all other people, over a protracted period of time.

We shall assume that the present collection of individuals who make up the United States constitutes a *bona fide* population. It originated in North America with the establishment of colonial settlements by British subjects from across the Atlantic Ocean in the early 17th century.

Many people from all over Europe, particularly from Germany, Russia, Austria-Hungary, Italy, Ireland later joined the English settlers. All of these early newcomers, together with the original Americans and enslaved Africans became the "primitive "members of the U.S. population.

How many actually came, and what impact they had on the formation and growth of the U.S. population will be discussed in Chapter 12. Nevertheless, the first official census of population in 1790 indicated the existence of some four million survivors. These are the 1790 Active U.S. population. It is not too far-fetched to presume that a number of migrants of probably twice that magnitude entered the U.S. during the century prior to 1790, thereby bringing the Effective Population to an estimated 8 million. This phenomenon is an example of the genesis of a most powerful population formation in the history of mankind.

In the ensuing 210 years, by year 2000, the engendering of domestic-born descendants by these original migrants and new migrants launched the population as a relatively closed birthing group and expanded the size of the Effective Population of the United States to a phenomenal 416 million souls. This consisted of an Active Population of 283 million and Inertial Births of 133 million.

Today, the population membership is an amalgam of off-springs from many distinct political states throughout the entire world. Most of their national identities, except for the most recent migrants, are submerged within the larger domestic-born population.

To be sure, a population of original natives existed in the geographic domain prior to the coming of the Europeans. An estimated 1.5 million subsisted in various hunter-gatherer and other primitive communal configurations. Today, they exist in relatively small numbers, but in a visibly identifiable mode within the larger population.

From the earliest beginnings of European settlements, a special brand of migrants was forcibly injected into the North American colonies as slaves. Between 1619 and 1790 an estimated 1.5 million were forcibly impounded into the North American colonies. Due to their original legal slave status and later legal "Jim Crow" existence, they currently form an identifiable subset within the bowels of the core population of the U.S. We estimate their Active Population to be 35 million in 2000; their Effective Population could well be close to twice that number.

Cultural Diversity

The fundamental conception to be pursued in our analysis is that the people of the U.S. exist today as *bona fide* population whose primitive beginnings can be traced to a specific period in history some four centuries ago. An extremely significant part of its dynamic is that it originated from a band of incipient English and other European migrants, and has continued to this day to ingest a steady stream of aliens from all over the world. It therefore inheres a number of population subsets of varying degrees of assimilation into the larger whole. Furthermore, the original inhabitants, as well as the former African slaves, exist as highly visible subsets within its bowels.

As a consequence of these factors there is a rich, diverse, and complex mixture of attributes distributed among members of the population. These include the traits which have come to be known in modern parlance as "cultural diversity", manifested in different languages, customs, religion, art, music, work skills, skin colors, and a host of other American traits.

It is also a consequence of such diversity that the potential always exists for unity as well as for conflict in the practice of citizenship. The clash of difference in national ethos, schisms within or among religious groups, competition for jobs and a place in society based on the concocted excuse of "race" are some of the practical grounds for endemic divisions within the population. These divisions are such as to generate social, political, and economic traumas in the implementation of political agendas of individuals and groups of population members.

Geographic Domain

The geographic domain of the U.S. population consists of the political subdivisions of the fifty states and the territories under the jurisdictions of the U.S. government. This space has been undergoing a steady process of expansion from the very beginning.

From a few scattered colonies of the Atlantic coast, the domain has come to occupy an area stretching westward from the Atlantic Ocean to the Pacific Ocean, and southward from the Canadian Border to Mexico and the Gulf of Mexico. Other territories have been annexed as a consequence of wars of conquest against the original Americans. Internecine wars against other European nations such as France and Spain have provided additions to the land arena. Wars against the Mexicans have provided vast stretches of land in the southwest and on the west coast. Political negotiation has brought in some valuable real estate from the famous Louisiana Purchase and other arrangements with Mexico, Spain, and England.

In 1790 the geographic domain encompassed some nine hundred thousand square miles. By 1840 it had expanded to 1.8 million square miles. It increased to 3.0 million in 1900 and reached a peak of 3.6 million square miles by 1986.

As a consequence of this dynamic expansion an environment was created that would affect the future attributes of the population.

Not without importance was the ready availability of an abundance of quite important non-human matter which would influence the specific types of materials necessary for the reproduction needs. Vast stores of minerals of all kinds, rich agricultural soil capable of accommodating a wide variety of food and other crops, temperate climate, vast reserves of timber in the rather extensive forest cover, abundance of fisheries, the effective possibility of significant transportation networks in the complex of mighty internal waterways like the Great Lakes and the Mississippi River, and the bordering oceans and gulf—all became significant factors in the creation of the attributes of the American people.

The Political State

The Political State which manages the system of reproduction of the population and its means of survival has undergone dynamic changes since 1790. From a set of proprietary colonies under the hegemony of British legal administrations, the Americans wrested independence as a result of a successful war of national liberation.

In 1776 independence was proclaimed; and by 1787 an effective government was established under what has been touted as an unprecedented written constitution.

At the outset of independence, the Political State put in place a system of Political Economy which operated in a dual mode. An agricultural system, based on African slave labor, dominated the southern states. This was a continuation of the colonial system of cultivation of tobacco and related crops.

In the other states a mixture of agriculture, industry, and trade dominated. These activities were evolving into a system of economy that would mimic that which had already developed in England and some of the countries of western Europe.

In time, a violent Civil War settled the dual mode of economy and established a unified Political State based on enforcement of the rules governing a system of Capitalist Political Economy. The essential dynamics of this system found initial implementation from earlier efforts by Alexander Hamilton and his cohorts during the Jefferson administration. This system persists to the present day.

Attributes stemming from acquiescence to the laws of the state have been implemented in the minds, and have colored the behavior of members of the population.

The system is based on (a) the acquisition of wage incomes in market institutions through the sale of one's ability to work; (b) acquisition of consumer goods in market institutions through the voluntary payment of money prices; (c) the production of non-human capital in privately owned capitalist business enterprises by wage workers; (d) production of population members in private family households; (e) private accumulation of capital by capitalists; and (f) social accumulation of dead population members by wage workers.

Creation of Special Traits

The capitalist Political Economy causes the creation of some special traits in the members of the population based on the repeated compliance with the rules of the game. Personal freedom is an endemic part of the rules. Population members must have personal freedom to participate or not to participate in market activities. They may exercise their own option to accept or not to accept a wage offer. On the other hand, a capitalist may exercise his freedom to offer or not to offer a job to an unemployed wage worker.

A worker must have private property rights in his person. At the same time, a capitalist must have private property rights in the ownership of his capital. Upon purchase of a consumer good, a worker must have the right to privately own and peaceably enjoy his purchased consumer good. At the same time, upon the purchase of the ability of a worker to work, a capitalist must have the right to privately own and peaceably use and enjoy what he has bought. The list of rules goes on.

The system generates selfishness on the part of all individuals in the pursuit of ownership of material goods—workers' abilities and capital on the part of capitalists; the right to a job and consumer goods on the part of workers. Hence the rule of self-interest and its attendant attributes color the behavior of individuals.

The system of capitalist Political Economy has no peer. It has caused the production of an immense quantity of goods which make up the gross domestic product. Millions of products of distinctive types issue from millions of capitalist establishments, guided strictly by private profitability of capitalists. But the production of any one of these goods is partly accomplished with the use of an extremely complex configuration of many distinctive forms of capital, in conjunction with a highly managed and cooperatively disciplined wage work force.

Moreover, the products are all interrelated one with another, some being the raw materials for the production of others. And the distributional mechanism entails national and even international markets. Thus, a tight web of interdependence is generated among all the members of the U.S. population who are engaged in producing and distributing these products.

The Political Economy also causes the production of living energies of wage workers. This is accomplished by the personal consumption of goods and services under the complete private control of the worker and his household members. Differences in quantities and types of goods as well as differences in methods employed within the different households generate wide differences in the distribution of skills and other attributes emanating from these households.

The capitalist system also generates specific types of incomes to members of the population. Money wages to workers and money profits to capitalists, in widely distributed amounts among individuals, are endemic attributes of the system. It is precisely these very wide variations in money incomes that make effective claims on the food and other materials which form the basis for the creation and honing of the traits of individuals.

Money profit income also determines the opportunity of capitalists to accumulate wealth. Thus, a wide measure of inequality in the ownership and quantity of accumulated capital wealth are characteristic marks of capitalism.

Great inequality in the ownership of resources is a trademark of the system. Among them is the distribution of wages between zero and very high levels, with most of the income in the lower end of the distribution, and quite a number at the zero level. Young workers just entering the market for employment find themselves in large numbers at the zero level of wages.

This sampling of attributes and their unequal distributions affect the individuals. It is absolutely important, therefore, to study the formation of the quantitative attribute of the population. People are the carriers of all the traits stemming from acquiescence to the rules and regulations of the capitalist political economy which reproduces the population and its means of survival, and consequently reproduces the individuals who make up the population.

The hypothetical population discussed in the first part of this work detailed the step by step constraints on individual behavior. When the constraints of the Political Economy impose their effects on the U.S. population member, the die is cast. The typical U.S. citizen goes about his activities mostly unaware of these limitations on his behavior. They appear to be natural consequences of being human. They seem to be built into his genetic makeup and not subject to personal change.

11

Birthing Backbone of the US Population

BIRTHS CONSTITUTE THE backbone of a population. Our consideration of the situation of the U.S. during the period 1790-2000 will concentrate on the actual pattern of births during that period. Chapter 2 generously supplies us with all the tools we need to accomplish this task.

Levels of Population Formation

The basic elements of a population are births. An appropriate aggregation of births, within a specified time-framework defines a corresponding population level.

There are three major levels of population formation. Total Population consists of all births during the time period from the first year of birth through the Current Year. Numerically, these years are represented by the upward ordered real positive integers from 1 to T, and the downward ordered positive integers from 0 to (T-1).

Initial Population consists of all births during the period ending 100 years prior to the Current Year. This period is represented by the upward ordered integers from 1 to (T-100), and the downward ordered integers from (T-1) to 100.

Finally, the Effective Population consists of all remaining births, taking place after 100 years prior to the Current Year, up through the Current Year. These years are represented by the upward ordered integers from (T-99) through T, and the downward ordered integers from 99 to 0.

As you can see, the three population levels split the entire time of formation of the population into two mutually exclusive, but adjoining sets of years, from 1 to (T-100), and (T-99) to T. The first group of years encloses the Initial Population. This population sets the initial conditions which the Effective Population uses as its starting parameters.

The second span of years encloses the Effective Population. This is the workhorse, the core of the entire population syndrome. It takes place within the Current Cycle.

Table 2.2 in Chapter 2, provides a good view of these levels of population structure.

Population Structure

Each major level of Population contains two groups of births, aggregated into strategic social actors, that play the decisive roles in Human Labor, which reproduces both the population and its non-human means of survival.

One of these groups of births is the Active Population. It is what the decennial census measures and is generally called “the population”. It is not, however, the population; it is the surviving group in the population. It is the repository of the living individual members. As such it has the capacity to autonomously exercise the individual conscious wills in a unified or collective or social manner.

It functions as the instrument of External Labor. In that role it uses up its energy and gets transformed into non-human material, the basis for maintenance of human life. It is also the active part of the subject of Internal Labor. In that role it uses up consumer goods and gets reproduced as the active component of the Effective Population.

The second group is Inertial Births. It is the passive, but quite essential member of the population. In its birth-state It functions as the object of Internal Labor. It is the catch-basin, the sink, the receptacle of Internal Labor into which consumer goods are absorbed, ingested, puffed into the Effective Population to enable their transformation into population members.

Population Arithmetic

Calculating the population structure is a fairly simple task. Recall from Chapter 2 that we are able to observe, from the vantage stage of the Current Year, the entire history of all the annual steps in the formation of the population. Let us state some of the relevant principles.

Every birth is encased in its annual Quantum Cocoon, marked with a unique ID, T(t,r). The elements of the ID are year of birth and age during the Current Year. If we assume that the numerical value of the Quantum Cocoon is bT, where b is a constant and T is the current year, the problem is solved, so long as we can ascertain the true value of b.

We now have that the value of the Quantum Cocoon is the "Velocity of Birth", the incremental birth of the Current Year.

And since the Current year is the sum of the specific year of birth plus the age during the Current Year of a Quantum Cocoon, the Velocity of Birth of the Current Year is also the "Velocity of Survival" plus the "Velocity of Death".

Aggregate Births over the span of years from 1 to T, is equal to the Total Population and is numerically equal to:

$$bT^2.$$

It follows that the Aggregate Births also equals the sum of Velocity of Survival plus the sum of the Velocity of Death.

$$bT^2 = (0.5)(b)(T)(T+1)] +(0.5)(b)[(T)(T-1)].$$

The first term on the right-hand side of this equation is the Active Population; the second term is the Inertial Population. The term on the left side of the equation is the Total Population.

Level of Population depends upon the span of years over which the aggregation is done. Initial Population is aggregated over the period prior to the Current Cycle. Effective Population is aggregated over the Current Cycle.

A general formula for calculating all three levels of population formation is captured by the following expression:

P = (0.5)(b)T^2 (+ or -) 50bT.

If the 50bT is subtracted from the first term on the right, we have the Initial Population.

Initial = (0.5)(b)T^2 – 50bT.

If the 50T is added to the first term on the right, we have the Effective Population.

Effective = (0.5) (b)T^2 + 50bT.

If we now add the Initial Population to the Effective Population, we have the Total Population.

Total = (0.5)bT^2.

We leave it to the reader to verify the validity of these formulas. They require no more than simple algebra to understand the calculations. And, all of this is made possible, due to the postulate of births being encased in Quantum Cocoons and glued on to a time frame in unique slots based on ID's which depend upon two characteristics of the Cocoon, year of birth and age during the Current Year.

We cannot overemphasize this point. The assumptions, existence postulates, and other simple hypothetical factors are relevant in helping us to decode the rather simple principles underlying the creation of otherwise complex appearing real world phenomena.

Table 11.2 exhibits a detailed set of formulas for computing the three levels of population formation, as well as the two components of each level—the Active Population and the Inertial Births.

Discovering the Value of "b"

The procedure for finding the value of the "b" parameter is guided by the properties of our hypothetical population when applied to birth data from the real U.S. world. The available birth data for the study period consisted of ninety-two annual births, from 1909 to 2000. Of these, only the last 50 or so were based on compulsory national birth registration. These data are detailed in the Appendix.

As of 2016, the year before this study was prepared for publication, we could have had another sixteen data points available, making for a total of 108. An ideal minimum should be 100. We settled with the 92 in order to be able to test the hypothesis against the census of 2000 as well as to make at least one prediction concerning the census of 2010. This would enable us to make tests against future censuses beyond those years near the end of the study.

In any event, the plan of attack on the constant of acceleration of births used the condition that the Velocity of Birth is the same time-dependent velocity for every Quantum Cocoon within the total population. At the same time, every Quantum Cocoon had its own "average velocity". We estimated the average velocities by computing the continuous 50-year averages from the 92 years' data. This yielded us 43 "average velocity" data points, one for each year 1958-2000.

We then tried to ascertain the degree to which these averages varied with time. We interpreted this to mean some acceptable change in the average of the 43 averages, divided by the corresponding change in time. Such a measure was readily available.

We considered the "change in the average annual births" to be represented by two "standard deviations", one above and one below the average of the 43 continuous 50-year averages. And the corresponding change in time was considered to be the 42 years of change of this average. This yielded the ratio of 458850 to 42, resulting in b = 10925.

A similar result for the case of migration yielded m = 1870.

These two numbers, b and m, when added together, give us a resulting combined constant for births and migrants of 12795.

In testing our computation of the Active Population against the U.S. census of population, the combined "b" parameter is the appropriate one to use, since the census contains both births and migrants. Nevertheless, in Chapter 12 we shall give a separate estimate of the impact of migration on the Active Population.

Decoding the Acceleration Constant

The parameter, b, is a powerful workhorse for calculating the value of the two basic groups of births which create a population out of individual births. These groups are the Active Population and the Inertial Births. One is the surviving members of the population; the other is the dead members of the population.

Because of the time-dependent manner in which births are created, aggregating resolves into summation of real positive integers. The specific aggregates of births which form our two strategic groups can be computed using simple formulas involving the "b" parameter.

Table 11.2 shows the computational formulas for estimating the specific groups for the Initial Population, the Effective Population, and the Total Population.

A corresponding set of tables at the end of this chapter applies these formulas to the estimation of the real world population groups for the Current Year 2000 for the United States. These show the actual computations for the Initial, the Incremental, the Effective and Total Populations. The separate and combined effects of births and migration are shown in these tables.

In Chapter 12 we will discuss the impact of Migration on population formation in the U.S. There, we will show that the impact can be determined by assuming that migration is likened to a supplementary system of creating population members that apes the process of birthing.

Our calculations will have the capacity to separate out the migration effect as well as to combine that effect with the birthing effect.

To test the efficacy of our hypothetical population, we present some data in one of the tables at the end of this chapter. In this table we compare the actual census data with our estimates of the Active Population.

Our estimates are to be viewed as hypothetical groups of births. We send a command to the real U.S. population engine to create the same corresponding real groups of births. We then compare our estimates with the U.S. result.

The degree of congruence between the two results will dictate whether or not we disprove the hypothesis presented in this work. If we do not disprove the hypothesis this does not mean that we have proved it to be true. All we can settle for is more confidence that we may be on the right track. It will take many such results to strengthen our belief that we are getting closer to the truth.

The computational formulas shown in our tables represent more groups than we can find in the national archives of the U.S. We will therefore command the US population engine to send us some results for the 1910 and the 2000 U.S. Censuses of Population. The sought after data are the number of surviving members of the U.S. population for the two years.

We also add the year 2010. This is the first census year outside of our study period. It is therefore interesting to see how our first "prediction" survives the test of reality.

The related estimates from our Tables are the Active Populations for 1910 and 2000. These represent the survivors during the years in question.

Herewith are the comparisons:

	Census	Hypothesis
1900	76,212,000	78,113,475
2000	281,421,906	283,473,225
2010	308,745,538	311,046,450

Let the judgement begin. Three cases are hardly a basis for such an important decision. However, our hypothetical results seem to suggest that we are in the same ballpark. Over a 100-year period we are riding along pretty well with the Census counts. This gives us some hope that the hypothesis was not rejected.

In addition, our estimate for 2010 appears to be in the same ball park as the census data.

Exact correspondence is not to be expected. It would seem that many events and circumstances could make for a lack of exact congruence between the two data sets. However, it is for future probes to uncover the factors which may account for the discrepancies between the two sets of data.

A table at the end of this chapter gives comparisons for all census years, 1790-2000. It also projects results for future census years, 2010-2050.

We did not expect that our hypothetical population would generate results equivalent to that of the real U.S. population for the first 100 years. However, we show the comparison of the Census data with that of our estimate of Active Population for the census years between 1790-1880.

Added data to Table 11.7 shows these comparisons. Between 1850 and 1880 (Time 40-90) our estimates come fairly close to those of the U.S. census data.

It appears that the comparison yields mixed results after 1880. Between 1890 and 2000, of the 12 comparisons of our Active Population with the U.S. Census, 6 cases show our estimates to overshoot the census by what appears to be significant amounts. The years involved are 1940-1990.

For the period 1940-1990 the hypotheticals are from six to 14 million greater than the actual data. We are not making any analysis to determine what may account for these differences. However, it is interesting to note that the Velocity of Migrant Entry was in a rising phase during these same years. Future analysis will have to determine if this, or other, factors are associated with the differences.

Finally, we note that for the two years 2000-2010 the actual data are within two million of the hypotheticals. Similarly, between 1890 and 1930 the hypotheticals are within three million of the actual data.

Our evaluation of the confrontation with reality does not come to final judgment. There are problems with the exactitude of census counts. We do not use this as an excuse for the lack of complete congruence with the hypothesis. Nevertheless, we believe that the hypothesis is in the ballpark. It appears to be a closely related series to the counts of the 22 U.S. censuses.

The usual excuse is that we need more research before a final judgment can be made. We do not take this stand. We feel strongly that we have created a hypothetical universe. It has been endowed with a number of novel attributes. Among them are the Quantum Cocoon, the nature of the time-frame, the unique slots for sorting the various Quantum Cocoons, the Gang of 2 and its connection to the Newtonian Laws of Motion, the specific way in which individual discrete population births transit a path through the various institutional constraints to create a population, the manner in which the population involves the joint reproduction of itself as well as its means of survival, the connection of these events to the creation of a Political Economy which is managed by a Political State, the Earth environment in which the Political State exists among all the types of political states in the world, and finally the nature of the Earthly basis for the existence of the births of new population member and all the trappings of life and death and reproduction that surrounds each individual who originates out of the earth and returns to its bosoms in a continuing dance between human and non-human earth matter.

Let the confrontation continue from the groundwork which we have laid down in this work.

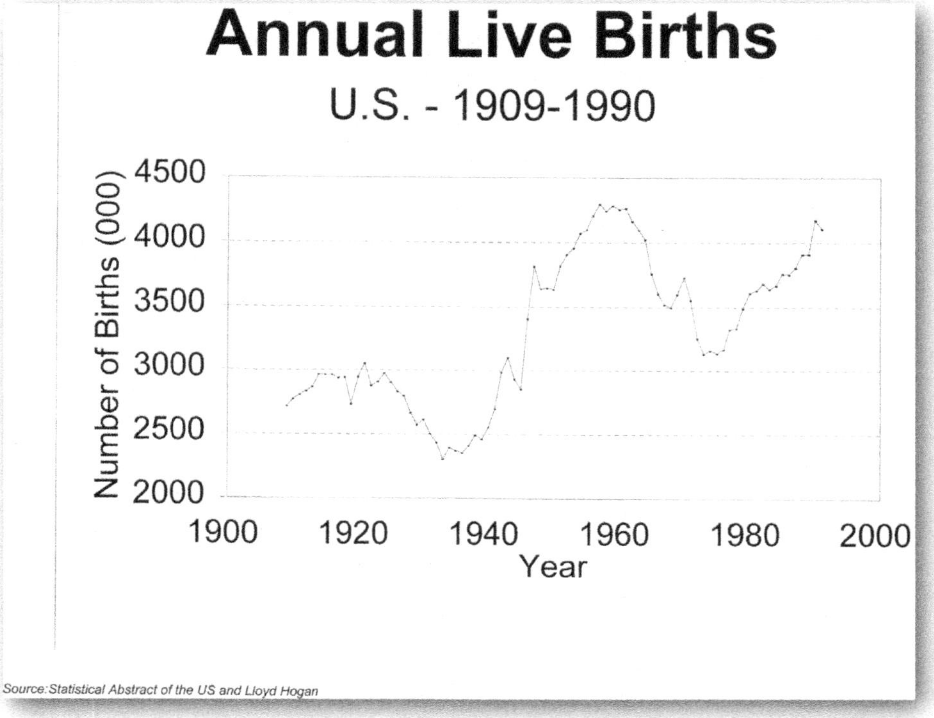
Annual Live Births
U.S. - 1909-1990
Number of Births (000)
4500
4000
3500
3000
2500
2000
1900
1920
1940
1960
1980
2000
Year
Source: Statistical Abstract of the US and Lloyd Hogan

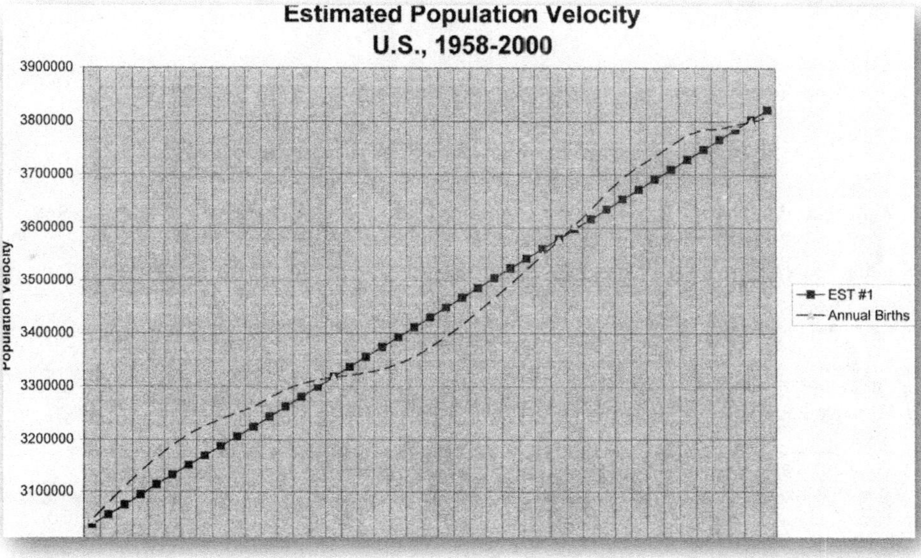
Estimated Population Velocity
U.S., 1958-2000
Population Velocity
3900000
3800000
3700000
3600000
3500000
3400000
3300000
3200000
3100000
EST #1
Annual Births

Table 11.2

POPULATION MORTALITY ARITHMETIC

By Type of Aggregated Births Over the Relevant Time Span

Aggregated Births	Inertial Pop	Active Pop	Total	Time Span
Initial Population	(T-100) (49.5)b	(0.5)(T-100)(T-99)b	(0.5)bT*2 – 50bT	1,(T-100)
Replaced Initial Pop	(T-100)(49.5)b	(0.5)(T-100)(T-99)b	((0.5)bT*2 -50bT	(T-99),T
Incremental Population	100(49.5)b	(100)(T-49.5)b	100bT	(T-99),T
Effective Population	49.5bT	(0.5)bT*2 + (0.5)bT	((0.5)bT*2 +50bT	(T-99),T
Total Population	(0.5)b(T)(T-1)	(0.5)b(T)(T+1)	bT*2	1,T

**COMPONENTS OF
INITIAL POPULATION MEMBERSHIP
UNITED STATES, 2000**

COMPONENT	YEAR OF BIRTH	SUB-COMPONENT	AGE*	SUB-TOTAL	TOTAL
Births	1790-1910		209-100		126183750
		Initial Inertial Births		59486625	
		Initial Active Pop		66697125	
Migrants	1790-1910		209-100		21598506
		Initial Inertial Migrants		10182150	
		Initial Immigrants		11416356	
TOTAL	1790-1910	Initial Population	209-100		147782256

Source: Calculated by the author, using parameters developed in the study.
*During the Year 2000.

COMPONENTS OF
INCREMENTAL POPULATION MEMBERSHIP
UNITED STATES, 2000

Table 11.3

COMPONENT	YEAR OF BIRTH	SUB-COMPONENT	AGE*	SUB-TOTAL	TOTAL
Births	1901-2000		209-100		229425000
		Delta Active Population		175346250	
		Delta Inertial Births		54078750	
Migrants	1901-2000		209-100		39270000
		Delta Immigrants		30013500	
		Delta Inertial Migrants		9256500	
TOTAL	1901-2000	Delta Initial Population	209-100		268695000

Source: Calculated by the author, using parameters developed in the study.
*During the Year 2000.

COMPONENTS OF
EFFECTIVE POPULATION MEMBERSHIP
UNITED STATES, 2000

COMPONENT	YEAR OF BIRTH	SUB-COMPONENT	AGE*	SUB-TOTAL	TOTAL
Births	1901-2000		209-100		355608750
		Active Population		242043375	
		Inertial Births		113565375	
Migrants	1901-2000		209-100		60868506
		Immigrants		41429856	
		Inertial Migrants		19428650	
TOTAL	1901-2000	Initial Population	209-100		416477256

Source: Calculated by the author, using parameters developed in the study.
*During the Year 2000.

Table 11.5

COMPONENTS OT TOAL POPULATION

UNITED STATES, 2000

COMPONENT	YEAR OF BIRTH	SUB-COMPONENT	AGE*	SUB-TOTAL	TOTAL
Births	1790-2000		209-0		481782510
		Inertial Births		239749135	
		Active Pop		242043375	
Migrants	1790-2000		209-0		82467000
		Inertial Migrants		41037150	
		Immigrants		41429150	
TOTAL	1790-2000		209-0		564259510
		Inertial		280786285	
		Active		283473225	

*Implicit Age. Any member with implicit age over 99 is reproduced during Current Cycle.

Table 11.6

Basic Birth Data

United States, 1909-2000

YEAR	TIME	AGE	BIRTHS	CUM(TIME)	CUM(AGE)	ACTIVE	VELOCITY
1909	119	92	2718	2718	310146	NA	NA
1910	120	91	2777	5495	307428	NA	NA
1911	121	90	2809	8304	304651	NA	NA
1912	122	89	2840	11144	301842	NA	NA
1913	123	88	2869	14013	299002	NA	NA
1914	124	87	2966	16979	296133	NA	NA
1915	125	86	2965	19944	293167	NA	NA
1916	126	85	2964	22908	290202	NA	NA
1917	127	84	2944	25852	287238	NA	NA
1918	128	83	2948	28800	284294	NA	NA
1919	129	82	2740	31540	281346	NA	NA
1920	130	81	2950	34490	278606	NA	NA
1921	131	80	3055	37545	275656	NA	NA
1922	132	79	2882	40427	272601	NA	NA
1923	133	78	2910	43337	269719	NA	NA
1924	134	77	2979	46316	266809	NA	NA
1925	135	76	2909	49225	263830	NA	NA
1926	136	75	2839	52064	260921	NA	NA
1927	137	74	2802	54866	258082	NA	NA
1928	138	73	2674	57540	255280	NA	NA
1929	139	72	2582	60122	252606	NA	NA
1930	140	71	2618	62740	250024	NA	NA
1931	141	70	2506	65246	247406	NA	NA
1932	142	69	2440	67686	244900	NA	NA
1933	143	68	2307	69993	242460	NA	NA
1934	144	67	2396	72389	240153	NA	NA
1935	145	66	2377	74766	237757	NA	NA
1936	146	65	2355	77121	235380	NA	NA
1937	147	64	2413	79534	233025	NA	NA
1938	148	63	2496	82030	230612	NA	NA
1939	149	62	2466	84496	228116	NA	NA
1940	150	61	2559	87055	225650	NA	NA
1941	151	60	2703	89758	223091	NA	NA
1942	152	59	2989	92747	220388	NA	NA
1943	153	58	3104	95851	217399	NA	NA
1944	154	57	2939	98790	214295	NA	NA
1945	155	56	2858	101648	211356	NA	NA
1946	156	55	3411	105059	208498	NA	NA
1947	157	54	3817	108876	205087	NA	NA
1948	158	53	3637	112513	201270	NA	NA
1949	159	52	3649	116162	197633	NA	NA

Page 1

1950	160	51	3632	119794	193984	NA	NA
1951	161	50	3820	123614	190352	NA	NA
1952	162	49	3909	127523	186532	NA	NA
1953	163	48	3959	131482	182623	NA	NA
1954	164	47	4071	135553	178664	NA	NA
1955	165	46	4097	139650	174593	NA	NA
1956	166	45	4210	143860	170496	NA	NA
1957	167	44	4300	148160	166286	NA	NA
1958	168	43	4246	152406	161986	152406	3048.12
1959	169	42	4286	156692	157740	153974	3079.48
1960	170	41	4259	160951	153454	155456	3109.12
1961	171	40	4268	165219	149195	156915	3138.3
1962	172	39	4167	169386	144927	158242	3164.84

Page 2

1963	173	38	4098	173484	140760	159471	3189.42
1964	174	37	4027	177511	136662	160532	3210.64
1965	175	36	3760	181271	132635	161327	3226.54
1966	176	35	3606	184877	128875	161969	3239.38
1967	177	34	3520	188397	125269	162545	3250.9
1968	178	33	3501	191898	121749	163098	3261.96
1969	179	32	3600	195498	118248	163958	3279.16
1970	180	31	3731	199229	114648	164739	3294.78
1971	181	30	3556	202785	110917	165240	3304.8
1972	182	29	3258	206043	107361	165616	3312.32
1973	183	28	3137	209180	104103	165843	3316.86
1974	184	27	3160	212340	100966	166024	3320.48
1975	185	26	3144	215484	97806	166259	3325.18
1976	186	25	3168	218652	94662	166588	3331.76
1977	187	24	3327	221979	91494	167113	3342.26
1978	188	23	3333	225312	88167	167772	3355.44
1979	189	22	3494	228806	84834	168684	3373.68
1980	190	21	3612	232418	81340	169678	3393.56
1981	191	20	3629	236047	77728	170801	3416.02
1982	192	19	3681	239728	74099	172042	3440.84
1983	193	18	3639	243367	70418	173374	3467.48
1984	194	17	3669	247036	66779	174647	3492.94
1985	195	16	3761	250797	63110	176031	3520.62
1986	196	15	3757	254554	59349	177433	3548.66
1987	197	14	3809	258363	55592	178829	3576.58
1988	198	13	3913	262276	51783	180246	3604.92
1989	199	12	3913	266189	47870	181693	3633.86
1990	200	11	4179	270368	43957	183313	3666.26
1991	201	10	4111	274479	39778	184721	3694.42
1992	202	9	4065	278544	35667	185797	3715.94
1993	203	8	4000	282544	31602	186693	3733.86
1994	204	7	3953	286497	27602	187707	3754.14
1995	205	6	3900	290397	23649	188749	3774.98
1996	206	5	3891	294288	19749	189229	3784.58
1997	207	4	3881	298169	15858	189293	3785.86
1998	208	3	3942	302111	11977	189598	3791.96
1999	209	2	3959	306070	8035	189908	3798.16
2000	210	1	4059	310129	4076	190335	3806.7
SUM			310129			7393888	147877.76
SIGMA			584.20246			11463.4545388	226.587489
AVG			3370.9674			171950.883721	3439.01767
Z			3421218			170609.4	3446474

Page 3

Table 12.3

BASIC MIGRANT DATA

United States, 1820-2000

YEAR	TIME	RAG	ANNUAL	CUM(TIME)	CUM(RAG)	50-YEAR SUM	VELOCITY
1820	30	180	8	8	66091	NA	NA
1821	31	179	9	17	66083	NA	NA
1822	32	178	7	24	66074	NA	NA
1823	33	177	6	30	66067	NA	NA
1824	34	176	8	38	66061	NA	NA
1825	35	175	10	48	66053	NA	NA
1826	36	174	11	59	66043	NA	NA
1827	37	173	19	78	66032	NA	NA
1828	38	172	27	105	66013	NA	NA
1829	39	171	23	128	65986	NA	NA
1830	40	170	23	151	65963	NA	NA
1831	41	169	23	174	65940	NA	NA
1832	42	168	60	234	65917	NA	NA
1833	43	167	59	293	65857	NA	NA
1834	44	166	65	358	65798	NA	NA
1835	45	165	45	403	65733	NA	NA
1836	46	164	76	479	65688	NA	NA
1837	47	163	79	558	65612	NA	NA
1838	48	162	39	597	65533	NA	NA
1839	49	161	68	665	65494	NA	NA
1840	50	160	84	749	65426	NA	NA
1841	51	159	80	829	65342	NA	NA
1842	52	158	105	934	65262	NA	NA
1843	53	157	52	986	65157	NA	NA
1844	54	156	79	1065	65105	NA	NA
1845	55	155	114	1179	65026	NA	NA
1846	56	154	154	1333	64912	NA	NA
1847	57	153	235	1568	64758	NA	NA
1848	58	152	227	1795	64523	NA	NA
1849	59	151	297	2092	64296	NA	NA
1850	60	150	370	2462	63999	NA	NA
1851	61	149	379	2841	63629	NA	NA
1852	62	148	372	3213	63250	NA	NA
1853	63	147	369	3582	62878	NA	NA
1854	64	146	428	4010	62509	NA	NA
1855	65	145	201	4211	62081	NA	NA
1856	66	144	200	4411	61880	NA	NA
1857	67	143	251	4662	61680	NA	NA
1858	68	142	123	4785	61429	NA	NA
1859	69	141	121	4906	61306	NA	NA
1860	70	140	154	5060	61185	NA	NA

12

Migrant Infrastructure of the U.S.

THE PRESENT DAY population of the U.S. originated out of the conquest of the native North American peoples and the usurpation of their lands by European settlers. This process began with the initial sorties by Columbus and his band of adventurers, who searched unsuccessfully for a westward sea route to India and its legendary treasures, but ended the quest in the American continent, then unknown to the Europeans.

Following Columbus, a number of explorers and their armies from Spain, Holland, France, and England scoured the North American continent. In some cases they established trading posts; in other cases they founded permanent settlements; and finally, they forged a variety of physical and institutional bases from which they launched the exploitation of the natives and their resources.

The most lasting impact of the Europeans, however, was the establishment of permanent colonies on the eastern shores of North America. Dramatic instances were the establishments of the colonies of Jamestown on the James River in Virginia and Plymouth on Cape Cod Bay in Massachusetts.

Almost two centuries following the establishment of Jamestown, a new independent American nation was forged out of the conquest of the natives, the expropriation of their lands, and a successful struggle against British colonial rule. The historical consequence was that the "primitive" cadre, in the form of European colonists, set into reproductive motion the inauguration of a crucially significant political entity on the world stage. And thus commenced the population of the United States of America.

Patterns of migration

A unique characteristic of the U.S. population is its relatively large migrant infrastructure. The incursions of migrants took place from the beginning and have continued relentlessly in considerable numbers each year to the present day. The U.S. Immigration and Naturalization Service (INS) reports that between 1820 and 2000 more than 66 million migrants were officially admitted to the United States from abroad. We estimate that between 1790 and 2000 a probable total of 82 million, together with their baggage of personal and social characteristics, now form an integral part of the quantitative and qualitative infrastructure of the current population of the United States.

We have no method of estimating the number of Migrants who entered what is now the United States between the founding of Jamestown and 1790. Nevertheless, the census of 1790 placed the survivors in 1790 at close to 4 million. This number of survivors is consistent with a Migrant total of 8 million during the century 1690 to 1790.

We hasten to note that during 1690 to 1790 a significant part of the Migrants were slaves from the African continent. While it is generally reported that such imports ceased after the outlawing of the slave trade in the early nineteenth century, there might well have been a good number of slave imports taking place after 1790 and before 1865. Contraband importations from the islands of the Caribbean may have provided a continuing source of the human material basis for the slave economy of the southern states.

Table 12.1 at the end of this chapter shows the official migration numerical entry data for the years 1820-2000.

These data conceal a rich mother lode of the patterns of migration. The migrants came from all over the world. But they came from the different continents and regions and countries at staggered intervals during the entire period in question. It was indeed a colorful vista of human diversification flowing relentlessly from abroad and entering into the cauldron of the U.S. population elixir, tinged with specific national-cultural signatures, in different time-sequential modes.

Europe and Canada were the major sources of these entrants. In the last few decades, however, Asia and Latin America have been dramatically increasing their contributions to the migrant stream.

Europe supplied 38.5 million immigrants during the period, comprising 58 percent of all migrants. These European migrants came primarily from six countries, which supplied close to ninety percent of the European contingent. These countries, in descending order of numbers supplied, are Germany (7.2 million), Italy (5.5 million), United Kingdom (5.3 million), Ireland (4.8 million), Austria-Hungary (4.4 million), Russia (3.9 million).

The Americas supplied 17.6 million, comprising 26.6 percent of all migrants. Most of these came from Canada and Mexico.

Asia supplied 8.8 million, comprising 13.3 percent of all migrants. A negligible amount came from the African continent (0.8 million) and from the rest of the world (0.8 million).

An important characteristic of the pattern of migration is its timing. Migrants from all the different countries and regions came in concentrated doses at different periods of time. Hence, the impacts of the different nationalities on the language, customs, and other characteristics of the population played themselves out in staggered periods of time. To measure the differential impacts we identify the 50-year contiguous period in which the country or area in question sent its largest number of migrants to the United States.

Table 12.2 at the end of this chapter gives these data for the major European countries and the major non-European areas.

The Irish impact was greatest during 1841-1890; fully 67% of all its migrants came to the U.S. during that period.

The Germans dominated the period 1851-1900, with 61.5% of its migrants entering the U.S.

The United Kingdom exerted its major influence during 1861-1910, with 54.3% of its total.

Austria-Hungary had its best effects during 1871-1920, with 93% of its total.

The Italians and the Russians supplied their greatest numbers during the period 1881-1930, with 84.1% and 84.4%, respectively.

Finally, Canada had its greatest impact during 1911-1960, with 51.8% of its total contribution.

It is thus seen that the influence of the European and European offshoot nations dominated during the period 1840-1930. The Latin American and Asian regions became the dominant sources of migrants from the middle of the 20th century to the present day.

The Latin-American countries exerted their greatest influence during the half-century from 1951-2000, supplying between 80%-95% of all their migrants. Similarly, the Asian countries made their most significant contributions during the period 1951-2000, supplying 79.3% of all their migrants.

The differential entry of Migrants from the many nations and groups of nations throughout the world demonstrates two essential points. Migrant impact of U.S. population is not only numerical, but it indicates the diversity of the non-quantitative attributes that the migrants brought. They came with practically all the major languages of the world. They worshipped in all the major religious sanctuaries. They brought various national and ethnic mores and folkways and general ways of life to the U.S. shores.

They also came in large numbers characteristic of the distinct groups. Hence, the impact of their native historic conditioning could be most effective among all the different groups in the U.S.

In any event, their total number, in conjunction with their other traits now constitute a significant part of the infrastructure of the U.S. population. It constitutes a force that cannot be ignored.

Figure 12.1 below gives a graphical portrayal of the annual migration into the U.S. from 1820 to 2000. No definitive temporal pattern is discernible in the annual migrant stream. The migrants came in annual quanta, averaging about 365,135 and ranging between a low of 8,000 and a high of 1,800,000. Within these limits, the migrant influx followed a very irregular pattern, with numerous peaks and troughs of differing magnitudes occurring at apparently random intervals.

The large and irregular stream of migrants over such an extended period of time has been widely credited with the relatively rapid numerical growth of the surviving members of the U.S. population. The surviving segment of the population rose from 3.9 million in 1790 to approximately 281.4 million in 2000. This multiplicative factor of more than 72 over the course of two centuries and a decade is unprecedented in population growth history.

The mechanism through which migrant entry influences such unprecedented growth in population survivors is not well understood. Sometimes the sheer number of entrants is believed to be identified with growth. On other occasions, the off-springs of the migrants are believed to represent an upward impact on the birth rate. In what follows we shall try to develop a precise description of the numerical pattern of migration so that a basis can be established to rationally gauge the probable mechanisms by which migration induces growth in the surviving population.

An unambiguous and accurate description of the pattern of migration requires a more rigorous analysis of the data beyond the raw annual statistics of migrant entry. Such an analysis entails the transformation of the raw data into conceptually more potent information.

The Quantitative Effect of Immigration

Migrant year of entry, and its residential age in the U.S. during the Current Year are the essential elements for sorting every annual group of Migrants. Such an ID, T(t,r) is practically the same used for sorting births. Hence, this is a method of integrating the Migrants into the population formation activities with the population members.

There are two possible ways of analyzing the effects of Migration on population outcomes. The Migrant is much like the Initial Active Population member. He was not born during the Current Period, but there he will die and there he will be reproduced as an Active Population member by a new birth.

As the years go by and as a consequence of population reproducing activities, some Migrants will succumb to death, others will survive. We designate the survivors as Immigrants; the dead Migrants are designated as Inertial Migrants.

During the Current Year, Initial Immigrants may be reproduced by (a) births from population members, (b) by births from Immigrants, or by (c) a mix of population members and Immigrants.

In the second and third cases the reproduced Migrant does not meet the definition of a *bona fide* population member. He may be classified as a special type of Migrant.

In the first case, the reproduced Migrant can meet the definition of a member in due time.

In practice, we assume that all three cases will take place. For analytic purposes, we cannot be faulted if we simply treat the Migrant effect as one in which it operates exactly like a process that apes the birthing process and thus produces a special type of resident. The total effect of birthing and migration can then be added to births to assess their total impact on population formation.

This amounts to interpreting the “b” parameter to be a sum of both the migrant contribution and the birth contribution. We will still be able to develop an estimate of the number of Migrants entering the population domain, broken down between Immigrants and Inertial Migrants.

Estimating the Migrant “m” Parameter

The very same procedures we used to estimate the “b” parameter for births is what we use to calculate the corresponding “m” parameter for Migrants.

The process is to convert the 181 annual Migrant data points into 132 contiguous 50-year averages. The average of these averages is computed to represent the constant velocity of Migration.

To ascertain if this overall average varies with time, we interpret twice its standard deviation as "the change in the average velocity of Migration"; and the "corresponding change in time" as the 131 (132 minus 1) data points in the calculation of the standard deviation.

This procedure yielded a value, m = 1870.

Table 12.3 shows the data used in the calculation of the migrant acceleration parameter.

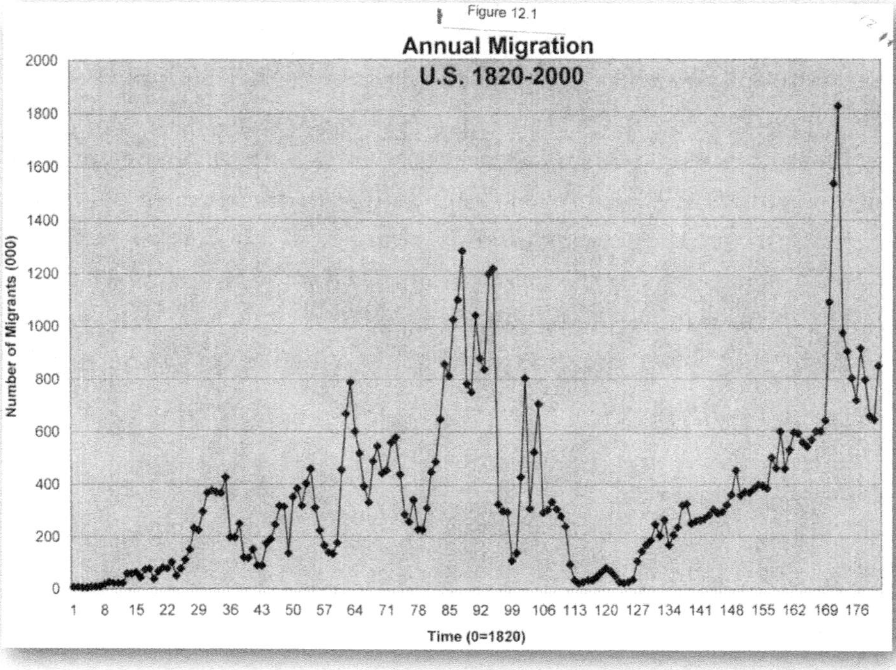
Figure 12.1
Annual Migration
U.S. 1820-2000
Number of Migrants (000)
2000
1800
1600
1400
1200
1000
800
600
400
200
0
1 8 15 22 29 36 43 50 57 64 71 78 85 92 99 106 113 120 127 134 141 148 155 162 169 176
Time (0=1820)

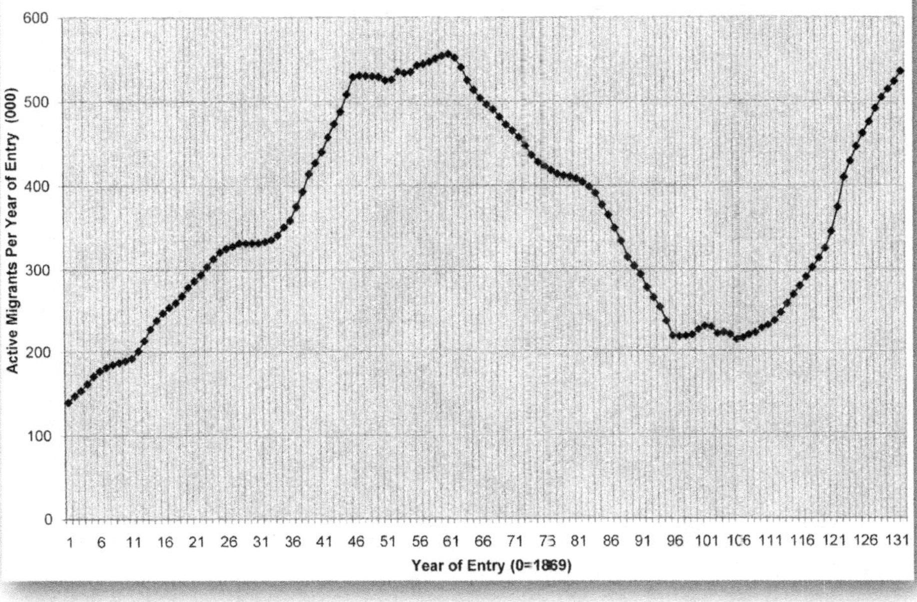

Figure 12.2

VELOCITY OF MIGRATION

U.S. 1859-2000

Table 12.1

TABLE 1. IMMIGRATION TO THE UNITED STATES: FISCAL YEARS 1820 - 2000

Year	Number	Year	Number	Year	Number	Year	Number
1820 - 2000	**66,089,431**						
1820	8,385						
1821-30	**143,439**	**1871-80**	**2,812,191**	**1921-30**	**4,107,209**	**1971-80**	**4,493,314**
1821	9,127	1871	321,350	1921	805,228	1971	370,478
1822	6,911	1872	404,806	1922	309,556	1972	384,685
1823	6,354	1873	459,803	1923	522,919	1973	400,063
1824	7,912	1874	313,339	1924	706,896	1974	394,861
1825	10,199	1875	227,498	1925	294,314	1975	386,194
1826	10,837	1876	169,986	1926	304,488	1976	398,613
1827	18,875	1877	141,857	1927	335,175	1976, TQ [1]	103,676
1828	27,382	1878	138,469	1928	307,255	1977	462,315
1829	22,520	1879	177,826	1929	279,678	1978	601,442
1830	23,322	1880	457,257	1930	241,700	1979	460,348
						1980	530,639
1831-40	**599,125**	**1881-90**	**5,246,613**	**1931-40**	**528,431**		
1831	22,633	1881	669,431	1931	97,139	**1981-90**	**7,338,062**
1832	60,482	1882	788,992	1932	35,576	1981	596,600
1833	58,640	1883	603,322	1933	23,068	1982	594,131
1834	65,365	1884	518,592	1934	29,470	1983	559,763
1835	45,374	1885	395,346	1935	34,956	1984	543,903
1836	76,242	1886	334,203	1936	36,329	1985	570,009
1837	79,340	1887	490,109	1937	50,244	1986	601,708
1838	38,914	1888	546,889	1938	67,895	1987	601,516
1839	68,069	1889	444,427	1939	82,998	1988	643,025
1840	84,066	1890	455,302	1940	70,756	1989	1,090,924
						1990	1,536,483
1841-50	**1,713,251**	**1891-1900**	**3,687,564**	**1941-50**	**1,035,039**		
1841	80,289	1891	560,319	1941	51,776	**1991-2000**	**9,095,417**
1842	104,565	1892	579,663	1942	28,781	1991	1,827,167
1843	52,496	1893	439,730	1943	23,725	1992	973,977
1844	78,615	1894	285,631	1944	28,551	1993	904,292
1845	114,371	1895	258,536	1945	38,119	1994	804,416
1846	154,416	1896	343,267	1946	108,721	1995	720,461
1847	234,968	1897	230,832	1947	147,292	1996	915,900
1848	226,527	1898	229,299	1948	170,570	1997	798,378
1849	297,024	1899	311,715	1949	188,317	1998	654,451
1850	369,980	1900	448,572	1950	249,187	1999	646,568
						2000	849,807
1851-60	**2,598,214**	**1901-10**	**8,795,386**	**1951-60**	**2,515,479**		
1851	379,466	1901	487,918	1951	205,717		
1852	371,603	1902	648,743	1952	265,520		
1853	368,645	1903	857,046	1953	170,434		
1854	427,833	1904	812,870	1954	208,177		
1855	200,877	1905	1,026,499	1955	237,790		
1856	200,436	1906	1,100,735	1956	321,625		
1857	251,306	1907	1,285,349	1957	326,867		
1858	123,126	1908	782,870	1958	253,265		
1859	121,282	1909	751,786	1959	260,686		
1860	153,640	1910	1,041,570	1960	265,398		
1861-70	**2,314,824**	**1911-20**	**5,735,811**	**1961-70**	**3,321,677**		
1861	91,918	1911	878,587	1961	271,344		
1862	91,985	1912	838,172	1962	283,763		
1863	176,282	1913	1,197,892	1963	306,260		
1864	193,418	1914	1,218,480	1964	292,248		
1865	248,120	1915	326,700	1965	296,697		
1866	318,568	1916	298,826	1966	323,040		
1867	315,722	1917	295,403	1967	361,972		
1868	138,840	1918	110,618	1968	454,448		
1869	352,768	1919	141,132	1969	358,579		
1870	387,203	1920	430,001	1970	373,326		

[1] Transition quarter, July 1 through September 30, 1976.

NOTE: The numbers shown are as follows: from 1820-67, figures represent alien passengers arrived at seaports; from 1868-92 and 1895-97, immigrant aliens arrived; from 1892-94 and 1898-1999, immigrant aliens admitted for permanent residence. From 1892-1903, aliens entering by cabin class were not counted as immigrants. Land arrivals were not completely enumerated until 1908. See Glossary for fiscal year definitions.

18

6

Table 12.2
MAXIMUM 50-YEAR MIGRANT ENTRY
By Country or Region
United States, 1841-2000

REGION OF ORIGIN	PERIOD OF ENTRY	MIGRANTS*	% OF REGION TOTAL
Ireland	1841-1890	3,222,969	67.4%
Germany	1851-1900	4,415,439	61.5
United Kingdom	1861-1910	2,859,784	54.3
Austria-Hungary	1871-1920	4,061,030	93.0
Italy	1881-1930	4,569,913	84.1
USSR	1881-1930	3,298,821	84.4
Canada	1911-1960	3,248,897	51.8
Mexico	1951-2000	5,299,311	86.3
Caribbean	1951-2000	3,185,268	86.5
Central America	1951-2000	1,275,724	94.7
South America	1951-2000	1,646,812	92.0
Asia	1951-2000	7,702,998	79.3
Africa	1951-2000	655,557	80.0

Table 12.3

BASIC MIGRANT DATA

United States, 1820-2000

YEAR	TIME	RAG	ANNUAL	CUM(TIME)	CUM(RAG)	50-YEAR SUM	VELOCITY
1820	30	180	8	8	66091	NA	NA
1821	31	179	9	17	66083	NA	NA
1822	32	178	7	24	66074	NA	NA
1823	33	177	6	30	66067	NA	NA
1824	34	176	8	38	66061	NA	NA
1825	35	175	10	48	66053	NA	NA
1826	36	174	11	59	66043	NA	NA
1827	37	173	19	78	66032	NA	NA
1828	38	172	27	105	66013	NA	NA
1829	39	171	23	128	65986	NA	NA
1830	40	170	23	151	65963	NA	NA
1831	41	169	23	174	65940	NA	NA
1832	42	168	60	234	65917	NA	NA
1833	43	167	59	293	65857	NA	NA
1834	44	166	65	358	65798	NA	NA
1835	45	165	45	403	65733	NA	NA
1836	46	164	76	479	65688	NA	NA
1837	47	163	79	558	65612	NA	NA
1838	48	162	39	597	65533	NA	NA
1839	49	161	68	665	65494	NA	NA
1840	50	160	84	749	65426	NA	NA
1841	51	159	80	829	65342	NA	NA
1842	52	158	105	934	65262	NA	NA
1843	53	157	52	986	65157	NA	NA
1844	54	156	79	1065	65105	NA	NA
1845	55	155	114	1179	65026	NA	NA
1846	56	154	154	1333	64912	NA	NA
1847	57	153	235	1568	64758	NA	NA
1848	58	152	227	1795	64523	NA	NA
1849	59	151	297	2092	64296	NA	NA
1850	60	150	370	2462	63999	NA	NA
1851	61	149	379	2841	63629	NA	NA
1852	62	148	372	3213	63250	NA	NA
1853	63	147	369	3582	62878	NA	NA
1854	64	146	428	4010	62509	NA	NA
1855	65	145	201	4211	62081	NA	NA
1856	66	144	200	4411	61880	NA	NA
1857	67	143	251	4662	61680	NA	NA
1858	68	142	123	4785	61429	NA	NA
1859	69	141	121	4906	61306	NA	NA
1860	70	140	154	5060	61185	NA	NA

Table 12.3a

1861	71	139	92	5152	61031	NA	NA
1862	72	138	92	5244	60939	NA	NA
1863	73	137	176	5420	60847	NA	NA
1864	74	136	193	5613	60671	NA	NA
1865	75	135	248	5861	60478	NA	NA
1866	76	134	319	6180	60230	NA	NA
1867	77	133	316	6496	59911	NA	NA
1868	78	132	139	6635	59595	NA	NA
1869	79	131	353	6988	59456	6988	139.76
1870	80	130	387	7375	59103	7367	147.34
1871	81	129	321	7696	58716	7679	153.58
1872	82	128	405	8101	58395	8077	161.54
1873	83	127	460	8561	57990	8531	170.62
1874	84	126	313	8874	57530	8836	176.72
1875	85	125	227	9101	57217	9053	181.06
1876	86	124	170	9271	56990	9212	184.24
1877	87	123	142	9413	56820	9335	186.7
1878	88	122	138	9551	56678	9446	188.92
1879	89	121	179	9730	56540	9602	192.04
1880	90	120	457	10187	56361	10036	200.72
1881	91	119	669	10856	55904	10682	213.64
1882	92	118	789	11645	55235	11411	228.22
1883	93	117	603	12248	54446	11955	239.1
1884	94	116	519	12767	53843	12409	248.18
1885	95	115	395	13162	53324	12759	255.18
1886	96	114	334	13496	52929	13017	260.34
1887	97	113	490	13986	52595	13428	268.56
1888	98	112	546	14532	52105	13935	278.7
1889	99	111	444	14976	51559	14311	286.22
1890	100	110	455	15431	51115	14682	293.64
1891	101	109	560	15991	50660	15162	303.24
1892	102	108	580	16571	50100	15637	312.74
1893	103	107	440	17011	49520	16025	320.5
1894	104	106	286	17297	49080	16232	324.64
1895	105	105	259	17556	48794	16377	327.54
1896	106	104	343	17899	48535	16566	331.32
1897	107	103	231	18130	48192	16562	331.24
1898	108	102	229	18359	47961	16564	331.28
1899	109	101	312	18671	47732	16579	331.58
1900	110	100	449	19120	47420	16658	333.16
1901	111	99	488	19608	46971	16767	335.34
1902	112	98	649	20257	46483	17044	340.88
1903	113	97	857	21114	45834	17532	350.64
1904	114	96	813	21927	44977	17917	358.34

Table 12.3b

1905	115	95	1026	22953	44164	18742	374.84
1906	116	94	1101	24054	43138	19643	392.86
1907	117	93	1285	25339	42037	20677	413.54
1908	118	92	783	26122	40752	21337	426.74
1909	119	91	752	26874	39969	21968	439.36
1910	120	90	1042	27916	39217	22856	457.12
1911	121	89	879	28795	38175	23643	472.86
1912	122	88	838	29633	37296	24389	487.78
1913	123	87	1198	30831	36458	25411	508.22
1914	124	86	1218	32049	35260	26436	528.72
1915	125	85	327	32376	34042	26515	530.3
1916	126	84	299	32675	33715	26495	529.9
1917	127	83	295	32970	33416	26474	529.48
1918	128	82	111	33081	33121	26446	528.92
1919	129	81	141	33222	33010	26234	524.68
1920	130	80	430	33652	32869	26277	525.54
1921	131	79	805	34457	32439	26761	535.22
1922	132	78	310	34767	31634	26666	533.32
1923	133	77	523	35290	31324	26729	534.58
1924	134	76	707	35997	30801	27123	542.46
1925	135	75	294	36291	30094	27190	543.8
1926	136	74	304	36595	29800	27324	546.48
1927	137	73	335	36930	29496	27517	550.34
1928	138	72	307	37237	29161	27686	553.72
1929	139	71	280	37517	28854	27787	555.74
1930	140	70	242	37759	28574	27572	551.44
1931	141	69	97	37856	28332	27000	540
1932	142	68	36	37892	28235	26247	524.94
1933	143	67	23	37915	28199	25667	513.34
1934	144	66	29	37944	28176	25177	503.54
1935	145	65	35	37979	28147	24817	496.34
1936	146	64	36	38015	28112	24519	490.38
1937	147	63	50	38065	28076	24079	481.58
1938	148	62	68	38133	28026	23601	472.02
1939	149	61	83	38216	27958	23240	464.8
1940	150	60	71	38287	27875	22856	457.12
1941	151	59	52	38339	27804	22348	446.96
1942	152	58	29	38368	27752	21797	435.94
1943	153	57	24	38392	27723	21381	427.62
1944	154	56	29	38421	27699	21124	422.48
1945	155	55	38	38459	27670	20903	418.06
1946	156	54	109	38568	27632	20669	413.38
1947	157	53	147	38715	27523	20585	411.7
1948	158	52	171	38886	27376	20527	410.54

Table 12.3c

1949	159	51	188	39074	27205	20403	408.06
1950	160	50	249	39323	27017	20203	404.06
1951	161	49	206	39529	26768	19921	398.42
1952	162	48	266	39795	26562	19538	390.76
1953	163	47	170	39965	26296	18851	377.02
1954	164	46	208	40173	26125	18246	364.92
1955	165	45	238	40411	25918	17458	349.16
1956	166	44	322	40733	25680	16679	333.58
1957	167	43	327	41060	25358	15721	314.42
1958	168	42	253	41313	25031	15191	303.82
1959	169	41	261	41574	24778	14700	294
1960	170	40	265	41839	24517	13923	278.46
1961	171	39	271	42110	24252	13315	266.3
1962	172	38	284	42394	23981	12761	255.22
1963	173	37	306	42700	23697	11869	237.38
1964	174	36	292	42992	23391	10943	218.86
1965	175	35	297	43289	23099	10913	218.26
1966	176	34	323	43612	22802	10937	218.74
1967	177	33	362	43974	22479	11004	220.08
1968	178	32	454	44428	22117	11347	226.94
1969	179	31	359	44787	21663	11565	231.3
1970	180	30	373	45160	21304	11508	230.16
1971	181	29	370	45530	20931	11073	221.46
1972	182	28	385	45915	20561	11148	222.96
1973	183	27	400	46315	20176	11025	220.5
1974	184	26	395	46710	19776	10713	214.26
1975	185	25	386	47096	19381	10805	216.1
1976	186	24	502	47598	18995	11003	220.06
1977	187	23	462	48060	18493	11130	222.6
1978	188	22	601	48661	18031	11424	228.48
1979	189	21	460	49121	17430	11604	232.08
1980	190	20	531	49652	16970	11893	237.86
1981	191	19	597	50249	16439	12393	247.86
1982	192	18	594	50843	15842	12951	259.02
1983	193	17	560	51403	15248	13488	269.76
1984	194	16	544	51947	14688	14003	280.06
1985	195	15	570	52517	14144	14538	290.76
1986	196	14	602	53119	13574	15104	302.08
1987	197	13	602	53721	12972	15656	313.12
1988	198	12	643	54364	12370	16231	324.62
1989	199	11	1091	55455	11727	17239	344.78
1990	200	10	1536	56991	10636	18704	374.08
1991	201	9	1827	58818	9100	20479	409.58
1992	202	8	974	59792	7273	21424	428.48

Table 12.3d

1993	203	7	904	60696	6299	22304	446.08
1994	204	6	804	61500	5395	23079	461.58
1995	205	5	720	62220	4591	23761	475.22
1996	206	4	916	63136	3871	24568	491.36
1997	207	3	798	63934	2955	25219	504.38
1998	208	2	660	64594	2157	25708	514.16
1999	209	1	647	65241	1497	26167	523.34
2000	210	0	850	66091	850	26768	535.36
		SUM	66091			2365406	47308.12
		MEAN	365.1436			17919.74	358.394848
		STDDEV	316.1155			6123.684	122.473675
		Z	489.969				378.744

13

Dynamics of Effective Population

THE EFFECTIVE POPULATION is the heart of the population. It is composed of all births during the Current Cycle. It is divided into two main groups—Active Population and Inertial Births.

The Active Population is the surviving segment, which is fueled by the exercise of the conscious wills of its members. It serves as the instrument of External Labor, that causes the transformation of human energy into non-human goods.

The Inertial Births are the dead segment. It plays a passive role as object of Internal Labor. It is the receptacle into which Consumer Goods are transmitted to Internal Labor, causing the transformation of non-human materials into human energy.

Structural Organization

The architectural plan of construction of the Effective Population is rather simple. First, it clones the Initial Population. It replaces the Initial Active Population, in exactly the same quantitative level, as Active Population. It also replaces the Initial Inertial Births, in exactly the same quantitative level, as Inertial Births.

This amounts to a quantitative incorporation of the population members of the past into the base of the current Effective Population.

But we should note that this base consists of some of the new births which take place within the confines of the Current Cycle. As such, it is possible that the births which form the base of the Current Population may have changed attributes from their predecessors. After all, they are different human beings, coming on board at a later period and therefore able to take advantage of learning from the past.

The next phase in the plan of the current Effective Population is to create some incremental births as Active Population, and some incremental births as Inertial Births.

The final format of the current Effective Population is seen to consist of two tiers, the replaced Initial Population and an increment to the Initial Population. It incorporates the past while adding more births to the quantitative membership. It insures the possibility of changes in the attributes of some of the members in all future population formations.

The formulas for calculating the Effective Population and its components are summarized below, where b=12795 (10925 birth effect and 1870 migrant effect).

E = Initial Pop + Incremental Initial Pop
Initial Pop = Initial Active + Initial Inertial Births
Initial Active Pop = b(T-100)(T-99)/2
Initial Inertial Pop = b49.5(T-100)

For the year 2000 (1790=0), the Initial Active Population is 78.1; Initial Inertial Births is 69.7; for a total Initial Population of 148.0. These amounts are in million.

We call attention to the 69.7 Initial Inertial Births. This is quite a huge number. In the studies of population and in popular statements, this number is ignored as part of the population. In our estimates it is about 90% of the Active Population, and over 47% of the Initial Population.

To dismiss such an important segment of the population is to discount the critical role that it plays in population formation. We must recall that among other things, it plays the role of object of Internal Labor. During the performance of this function, it undergoes its "death" state, while capturing the consumer goods for transformation into the human population. Its accumulation is the start of External Labor. In this role, it undergoes its "birth" state, while releasing its grip on Active Population to enable its escape to act as agent of External Labor.

In short, Inertial Births is a major player in the execution of Human Labor, the process which reproduces the population as well as its non-human means of survival. Could it be that this part of the Effective Population behaves like "dark matter"?

Increment to Initial Population is estimated by

Incr Active Population=b(100)(T-49.5)T
Incr Inertial Births = b(100)49.5bT

Numerically, for year 2000, Incremental Active Population is 205.4; Incremental Inertial Births is 63.3; and Incremental Initial Population is 268.7.

The same remarks above, concerning the Initial Population and its components, applies to the Incremental Population and its components. Both living and dead groups of births embody critical elements of human populations. They are the creators of Human Labor, the process which enables the reproduction of the population and its material means of survival.

A summary statement of the formula for computing the Effective Population and its components follows:

E = 0.5bT^2 + 50bT
A = 0.5bT^2 +0.5bT
I = 49.5bT

Table 13.1 shows the estimates of Effective Population for the U.S. for the years 1890 to 2000. It also shows the projected estimates for the decennial years 2010 through 2100.

The projected estimates will obviously depend on conditions which are implied from our study, including the critical role of the pattern of Migration which was endemic to the period from 1790 to 2000. In light of possible unprecedented reversal of past Migration policies by the Political State, these estimates must be viewed with caution.

Population in Motion

It should be obvious by now that the Effective Population is a moving event. The motion can be viewed in many ways. One way is to fix on a specific Initial Population as an unchanging quantitative event. From then on, just keep adding an increment of 100 years to this base, then add successive 100-year increments to the results.

This method yields complete cyclical changes, following a pattern: base 1, plus increment 1; plus increment 2; plus increment 3; ....; etc.

This same procedure may be applied using any year as base period starting point, and then keep adding successive 100 year increments to successive computations. In this way, it is possible to develop a data set of Effective Population for every single year in any given interval of years.

Starting with a known year, this make it possible to project the Effective Population for any number of years into the future.

An Exercise in Population Dynamics

It should be obvious by now that the Current Year is a moving feast. It follows that the Current Cycle is an annually moving entity. In other words, one may estimate the Effective Population for successive one year changes in the Current Year. Or it may be estimated for a specified 10-year change in the Current year, etc.

The dynamics of Effective Population are embedded in the relationship between births, survivors, and death, as follows: births = survivors + deaths.

It should be noted that during the Current Year the sum of the year of birth and age during the Current Year is equal to the Current Year for every specific year of birth throughout the history of population formation. This common equal value means that the Velocity of Birth for the Current Year is exactly the same for every specific year of birth in the population.

The Effective Population is not an inert object. It is a viable, active group of living human beings, exercising their conscious will, to create a potent entity of its own social identity distinct from the individuals who make it up.

It is in constant motion, producing new births, converting them into living and dead members, who reproduce the population as well as its means of survival.

These activities continue apace at a frequency of one year, based on a 100-year cycle. Let us illustrate.

For time 150 (year 1790=0), the Effective Population of the U.S. is 239.9 million, by our estimate. With the passage of one year, it will shed 2.3 million members, replace them with an equal number of births, and add increment of 2.4 million births.

If now we consider a change of a complete cycle to time 250, it will send 239.9 million back into the past generations; it will create 559.8 million out of the future generations to form the new present generations.

The 559.8 million will be a complete refreshing of the membership. This will be accomplished by replacing the original 239.9 million Initial Population, consisting of 145 million Active Population and 95 million Inertial Births with 401 million Active Population and 158 million Inertial Births.

These numbers are quite impressive. Our birthing engine and its accompanying machinery that produces the goods and services to accommodate them in their quest for survival is a potent device. These numbers tell the story of what we can expect between years 1940 and 2040.

Effective Population as Analytic Tool

Our hypothetical model of the Effective Population may not be in perfect congruence with the real population of the United States. Nevertheless, all is not a losing effort. We can still salvage some good from the arduous work involved in decoding some of the underlying issues in population formation.

More particularly, the hypothetical work can serve as a model, a tool for analyzing problems in population formation. One critical example is to consider the large deviations between the real world and the hypothetical world. This difference may be a flag that the difference is caused by some specific systematic occurrence.

For example, in projecting the Effective Population, it is important whether or not we use the known values of the Initial Population. If so, then the test of the hypothesis would turn on assessing the "predicted" change in the elements of the Effective Population, rather than in the actual magnitudes.

This procedure, however, would depend upon whether or not we have confidence in the "actual" initial values. In our case, the Census is the best measure we have for testing the Active Population. While the U.S. has developed a very sophisticated method of census taking, nevertheless, there have been questions concerning undercounts of minorities and poor in the largest cities of the nation.

The dictum is still to be honored that we must know what it is that we are studying before we can explain why it is what it is. There is always a temptation to explain a phenomenon and propose policy actions before we even have a fair idea of what the phenomenon is. We call this rushing to judgment, or "putting the cart before the horse". It is premature prescription for resolving a malady, and may well lead to fatal results.

We conclude this section of the work with Table 13.1 displaying our projected estimates of the U.S. Effective Population and its components for the decennial years 2000-2100.

Table 13.1

EFFECTIVE POPULATION COPONENTS
U.S. 1890-2100

YEAR	TIME		ACTIVE	INERTIAL	EFFECTIVE
1890	100		64615	63335	127950
1900	110		78113	69669	147782
1910	120		92892	76002	168894
1920	130		108949	82336	191285
1930	140		126287	88669	214956
1940	150		144903	95003	239906
1950	160		165000	101336	266136
1960	170		185975	107670	293645
1970	180		208431	114003	322434
1980	190		232165	120337	352502
1990	200		257180	126671	383850
2000	210		283473	133004	416477
2010	220		311046	139338	450384
2020	230		339899	145671	485570
2030	240		370031	152005	522036
2040	250		401443	158338	559781
2050	260		434134	164717	598806
2060	270		468105	171005	639110
2070	280		503355	177339	680694
2080	290		539885	183672	723557
2090	300		577694	190006	767700
2100	310		616783	196339	813122

Part III
The Future of Population Analysis

14

Generalizing The U.S. Experience

THE RESULTS OF this study should yield a better understanding of the various types of populations residing in all the different types of Political States in the world. The different types, based on the evolutionary development of the Political Economy, immediately come to mind. Primitive Communal, Slave, Share-cropping, Capitalist Political Economies would appear to differ with respect to the parameters necessary to construct their respective populations.

Among other parameters which seem to determine the different types, two stand out as being of signal importance. The time-frame and its role in defining the Velocity of Birth is one. A second is the determination of the acceleration parameter, b.

Concepts of Time and Motion

We adopt the Aristotelian definition of time as "a measure of motion". We interpret this to mean that time does not move; it is quite stationary, being associated with some three-dimensional thing that does the moving. We go a little further in our assumptions.

Time is likened to a continuous frame which is calibrated into equal units. It is a framework that encloses an object in three-dimensional space. It is analogous to a ladder, with each rung of unlimited width, of one unit length, and of unlimited height.

The left side rungs of the ladder are labeled with an ordered upward sequence, mimicking the positive real integers from 1 to T. On the right side of the ladder the related rungs are labeled in a downward ordered sequence, mimicking the real positive integers from 0 to (T-1).

Motion is conceived to be an attribute of some tangible thing which has the ability to autonomously act, to be alive, to change.

As a new object appears on the scene it is glued on to the topmost unoccupied rung of the ladder; this rung becomes its mate forever. Thus, an object of the same genre keeps ascending the ladder in equal discrete units of time.

The span of upward motions prior to the current upward motion are matched by the span of downward motions. Hence, the last upward motion represents an increment to the span of all motions to date.

Different kinds of motion of an object are identified with differences in the "velocity" of the object. It is the incremental change in motion associated with one unit of time.

Linear velocity is one type, indicating that the motion is quadratic.

Constant velocity is a second type, indicating that the motion is linear.

Zero velocity is a third type, indicating that the object is not moving with time. This case needs elaboration. The object is moving in a cyclical manner, maintaining its quantitative state at the end of each cycle. It can be related to time, however, by converting its angle of motion into an appropriate phase angle.

These different types of velocities could well depict different stages in the evolutionary development of a specific population.

The first stage is one of angular motion. This is the case of zero Velocity, a condition independent of time. The population is born during a given cycle. Its quantitative level of births is the same from cycle to cycle. This describes a population with zero growth.

The second stage is one in which both zero and constant Velocity prevail. Its birth effect is to clone the base cycle and add an amount generated by the constant velocity during the Current Cycle. During the ensuing cycle, the total births amount to cloning the births of the preceding cycle, including the base cycle.

The third stage is one in which all three Velocities hold sway. Base cycle maintains its constant quantity. Constant velocity adds a constant amount to the base cycle. Linear velocity adds an incremental growth to the base cycle.

It should be noted at once that the type of motion in each case is the aggregation of the Velocity.

It appears that we have discovered a way of identifying different stages in the evolution of a particular Political Economy. The presumption is that for a given Political Economy, it goes through a sequence of different types of velocities over time.

First, it follows a zero velocity. This phase is then followed by a combination of zero velocity and constant velocity. It is finally followed by a combination of zero, constant, and linear velocity.

Perhaps, the names that we give these three types should be novel, quite different from the lexicon of the past. In any event, the three cases stand firm and should help us in the quest for a more accurate analysis of population types.

In the case of the United States we have found this classification to be very useful in identifying the zero year in its time frame. We fixed on the year 1790 as year zero in its time frame, precisely because we found this year to be the start of sustained linear growth in its population.

Since the U.S. population is a linear growth case, it simultaneously undergoes all three types of Velocities.

Classifying other real world populations on the basis of the three types of Velocities, will help in their analyses.

Birthing is a good example of the concept of motion in practice. Its occurrence takes place in a continuous sequence. If we identify each occurrence by its annual entry, a direct connection is made to time.

Individual births arise from an operation of two adults, within a family setting. Upon birth the new population member is impounded into a Quantum Cocoon, consisting of all individuals born during a given Current Year.

As a new annual set of births appears it is assigned a slot in the time-frame, designated with an unique ID, T(t,r), where t is the year of birth and r is the age during the Current Year, T.

For any given span of contiguous years, the Velocity of Birth is a two-pronged vector, one going up and the other going down, with both spanning the same set of years. Multiplying the Current Year, T, by a fixed number, b, gives the velocity of birth, q(T). At the same time, this velocity is the sum of two associated velocities--the Velocity of Survival, q(t) and the Velocity of Death, q(r).

We are witnessing the essence of what motion means in the context of population formation. A new discrete Quantum Cocoon, consisting of a number of discrete individual population members, comes into existence annually. It occupies a new position at the top of the time-frame.

The effect of this one new annual birth cocoon is to cause an incremental one year upward movement in the set, t, of "year of birth" cocoons, with zero increment in the age of the new cocoon. This means that the year of birth is unchanged for every pre-existing Quantum Cocoon, but each experiences an incremental one year of age downward.

In sum, the new Quantum Cocoon causes an incremental year of upward movement in the set of "year of birth", while leaving unchanged the specific "year of birth" for pre-existing Quantum Cocoons. At the same time, the set of "age during the Current Year" is increased by one year. Each of these Quantum Cocoons therefore experiences an incremental year of age.

An additional year of age is added to the ID of each pre-existing Quantum Cocoon with every new annual birth. The net result is that during the Current Year, the incremental change in births is equal to bT, where "b" is a constant and T is the Current Year.

This simple result is also the same for every specific year of birth, t. This remarkable result is so because the sum of the two ID markers, t and r, is always and everywhere identically equal to the Current Year, T.

At the same time, each individual within its Quantum Cocoon, is exercising its conscious will to perform all kinds of population reproducing activities of different types, at different speeds, at different times, probably unaware of the socializing actions of Human Labor forging a specific Political Economy out of the aggregation of the Quantum Cocoons of which it is a very, very negligible part.

In all this, motion is executed by each quantum of births. A movement upward and a simultaneous movement downward, of discrete Quantum Cocoons, consisting of discrete population members, on an unmoving continuous time scale, in discrete time units, is the result.

This is heady stuff. In the United States during the year 2000 we witnessed an average Quantum Cocoon of 4.16 million births, made up of 2.83 million upward moving survivors and 1.33 million downward moving deaths.

If this doesn't boggle the mind, the 4.16 million discrete individuals in the Quantum Cocoon were born to approximately 4.16 million families. Each of these families harbored about five members, each residing in its own unique Quantum Cocoon, within each of millions of different families.

What the time-dimension has done is to make it quite simple to aggregate the births that form groups of Active Population Members and groups of Inertial Births, who are the principal actors in the reproduction of the Effective Population and the reproduction of the non-human means of survival of the population.

These millions and millions of interacting individuals, carry out their daily tasks of survival, creating new traits, honing their old traits, and otherwise going about the difficult business of maintenance of their lives independently of their cohorts. And yet, the astute observer can view this apparently complex adventure as a very simple scheme of aggregating a contiguous set of Quantum Cocoons. The description of this apparently extremely complicated event is as easy to digest as a piece of apple pie.

Experimental Possibilities

We have taken a look at three randomly selected populations which are observed to exhibit linear velocity in population formation.

The African American Active Population went from three-fourths of a million in 1790 to 35.0 million in 2000 and 38.9 million in 2010.

The Chinese Active Population went from 583 million in 1953 to 1,266 million in 2000, and 1,340 million in 2010.

The Indian Active population went from 439 million Active Population in 1961 to 1,029 million in 2001 and 1,210 million in 2011.

A rather quick analysis of the structure of any one of these populations is to ascertain two critical parameters—a time frame, t, and the acceleration parameter, b.

The Active Population is calculated by the following formula.

A(T) = 0.5bT^2 + 0.5bT

To estimate "b", one would simply use the formula:

Estimate of b = 2A/(T)(T+1).

We arbitrarily computed this measure for the six years 1870-1890, and 1990-2010 for the African American Population. The average result was 1543.

Testing the estimated Active against the actual Census figure gave the following results:

YR	EST	CEN
1870	5.0	4.9
1880	6.3	6.6

1890	7.8	7.5
1990	31.0	30.0
2000	34.1	34.7
2010	37.5	38.9

These comparisons appear to be quite related. However, we place no significance to the apparent equality between them. A more systematic choice of the years used in the computation of the "b" parameter would be needed. Furthermore, we should go through as thorough a study of the data for the African American Population as we did for the U.S. as a whole.

Nevertheless, what we try to demonstrate here is that it is possible to do the kind of study of the African population as we did for the U.S. population. From what we know about the African Population we believe that it is a *bona fide* subpopulation within the bowels of the larger U.S. population. A complete analysis of this case would contribute to our understanding of how to describe this type of phenomenon.

Estimating the value of T, using the value of b for the U.S. is accomplished by solving a quadratic equation. This procedure is fairly simple and gives us a practical method of applying the results of the U.S. to other populations, for which we have good census data.

We tried this procedure for the cases of India and China. The results were 46434 and 57135, respectively. The indication is that these two populations have acceleration coefficients between 4 and 5 times that of the U.S.

Again, we place no critical importance to these results. We merely indicate how one may go about making the estimates to use in a preliminary way to start a detailed study of the population in question.

India and China have the largest Active Populations in the world. No other Active Population comes close. A well-designed study that considered all the important circumstances in which these population survived is called for. It far exceeds the hopes of this study.

There are many more experiments that we may try with different populations to gather more insights into population formation issues.

In each case, however, our experiments should insure that we are dealing with *bona fide* populations.

We have used the Political State of the United States as the basis for identifying a population. In general, of course, this assumption may not be valid. It is possible that many distinct populations, at different evolutionary stages in their development, may exist within a Political State. An example is a State like Nigeria. It consists of many populations. But its boundaries were set as an administrative convenience of the former Colonial government.

To complicate matters, the possibility exists that a population can be grounded in more than one Political State. The Jewish people come to mind in this regard.

There is no doubt that there will be many difficulties to be encountered in the pursuit of clarity and understanding of what a population is. However, it is absolutely a must proposition that we should know precisely what a population is before we can begin to explain why a population is what is.

Beware of the policy prescriptions of those who know not what a population is. They may be proposing snake oil for the cure of a serious population malady. Worst of all, the proposed cure may be a fatal dose of poison.

15

Lessons Learned from the Study

The analysis of population origin, formation, growth, development, and final outcome has been a long, arduous, and lonely venture inside the secret trappings of mother earth. At the end of the trail we have come to believe that we are beginning to get a glimpse into the architectural plan from which the earth engineers the reproduction of itself.

INDEED, WE BELIEVE that the earth is a living organism; it is constantly engaged in a process of autonomously reproducing itself; and each unique type of material of which it is composed is likewise undergoing its own process of reproduction, by mimicking that of the earth itself.

We further believe that the principle underlying the reproductive process is a very simple one. However, when applied to relatively small pieces of earth matter, like a specific population the individual elements of such matter appear to be participating in a very complex and random dance, without following any reasonably identifiable stepping pattern. For example, individual population members appear to be doing every conceivable activity at the same time.

Throughout the geographic expanse occupied by the population, at one and the same time, different individual population members are simultaneously eating, sleeping, negotiating for a job, working at a particular job, being transported from home to work, being entertained at a hip-hop concert, being formally schooled at a kindergarten, being schooled at a university, being schooled at a central high school, shopping at the grocers, shopping at the mall, wearing every type of clothing imaginable, and on and on and on.

To the unknowing observer this impossible example of multi-tasking or multi-states attribute is a mirage, or perhaps such reality is too complex to fathom. How could one individual do all these things at the same time? Perhaps, one needs something like a quantum theory to describe this kind of phenomenon. Not to worry. It can be understood by a peeking into mother earth's knowledge bin.

In what follows we summarize some of the principles followed by mother earth in reproducing herself as well as reproducing all of her constituent elements. The overriding presumption is that if the earth is reproducing herself, then every part of the earth is an integral part of that reproduction. The reproduction of the whole is composed of the many reproductions of its many parts. The unifying principle that binds the reproduction of the parts into the reproduction of the whole is the appropriate descriptive hypothesis we have tried to uncover.

The Gang of 2

Aristotelian logic proclaimed that "...a thing cannot be and be at the same time in the same place and in the same respects". Over the years we have rejected this dictum. Our experience exhibited quite a different interpretation of the facts. We have observed that whenever an object is in motion, it is the result of two opposite elements bound together in a synthesizing dance.

A "Unity of Opposites" is the name that we formerly used to describe an object in motion. Today, we give it a new label—Gang of 2. It appears very often in the real world. It dominates the hypothetical realm of population formation developed in this work.

A scheme of our hypothesis may be portrayed by a sequentially related series of specific Gangs of 2. We begin with mother earth. It is a synthesis of (a) human earth matter and (b) non-human earth matter. This is earth matter in motion.

The earth then gives rise to a living baby, which is a union of (a) male adult parent and (b) female adult parent.

The baby possesses a human life, which is a union of (a) year of birth and (b) age.

The aggregation of human lives is Births, which is a synthesis of (a) survivors and (b) deaths.

Births are the active agents in the creation of Human Labor, the union of (a) Internal Labor and (b) External Labor.

Human Labor gives rise to a Political Economy, which is a unity of (a) human population and (b) non-human matter.

The Political State arises to manage the Political Economy. It is the synthesis of (a) working class as a type of property owners and (b) the ruling class as a different type of property owners.

Finally, the Political State is grounded in earth space. In the case of human population earth space is composed of (a) human earth matter and (b) non-human earth matter.

This sequence of events illustrates the concrete act of motion on a grand unified scale of the earth being transformed into the earth, by way of the reproduction of the human population as human population.

The human population starts with the creation of a new baby out of the earth, by way of its adult parents. Through many Gang of 2 motions, it creates a human population, consisting of Active Population and Inertial Births. The Active Population first dies and is then reproduced as Current Active Population. The Inertial Births are first born and then are reproduced as Current Inertial Births.

The essential act of reproduction of the human population involves numerous applications of the Gang of 2, thereby exhibiting movement or change, from one state of being to another state of being. The secret of motion seems to be the act of reproducing the state of being itself—preserving the form and attributes of the object in motion, while providing for possible change in quantity and non-quantitative attributes of such an object.

Hence, the Gang of 2 is the act of motion itself, the dynamic tension between two opposing elements, resulting in the formation of a synthesis. One member of the synthesis undergoes a transformation into its opposite companion.

Depending upon which one dominates the action, the synthesis may have a form that is (a) the same as one of its elements, or (b) the form of the other element, or (c) a form that combines the properties of both elements, or (d) a form that is independent of both of its elements.

If the Gang of 2 is a more general principle than its role in population formation, we should observe its operation in other areas. We believe that it has played a critical role in the thinking of the physical and biological scientists for at least four centuries. Newton's Laws of Motion come to mind as a high-profile example.

Newton's Third Law and The Gang of 2

Every school child soon gets exposed to the famous Laws of Motion of Newton. It should become apparent that motion and Gang of 2 are the same thing. Motion takes place in various ways, based on the velocity of the moving object. Velocity comes in three flavors—zero, constant, and linear.

Three combinations of these are admissible in any given case. These are (a) zero alone, (b) zero combined with constant, and (c) a combination of zero, constant, and linear. These three possibilities are symptoms of stages in the development of a given population. The assumption is that the first stage is the zero velocity motion; followed by a second stage of zero-constant velocity; and finally followed by a zero-constant-linear velocity stage.

Our hypothetical population demonstrates the existence of Newton's Third Law. The Effective Population is built with (a) cloning of the Initial Population, and (b) creating an increment to the Initial Population.

The clone moves at a constant velocity from the Initial Population. The increment moves at a linear velocity from the cloned Initial Population to the increment. The zero-velocity is implicitly there somewhere.

Before year zero, the population moves at an angular velocity. It then maintains the same quantitative magnitude from cycle to cycle. If we convert the angular velocity to a phase angle, the constant cyclical quantity becomes a wave form, superimposed on the Effective Population, with an amplitude of its constant measure.

The Velocity of Birth is composed of two parts—the Velocity of Survival and the Velocity of Death. The Velocity of Birth moves in two opposite directions as Gang of 2 members of the synthesized Velocity of Birth. These velocities are all linear in the case of the U.S. However, they incorporate the constant velocity in the cloning of the elements of the Initial Population.

The existence of the zero velocity (the angular velocity) of the apparent pre-temporal stage is an active population of approximately four million. This is consistent with a pre-1790 Effective Population of eight million. This number of population members is the rotating members of the velocity of motion, indicating a plus or minus value addition to the Effective Population. From the standpoint of the arithmetic, the general effect on the numbers is zero. Hence, we did not include it in the analysis. But it is still there and there it will remain forever, playing an essential role in the United States population formation and change.

Creative Role of Death

We have indulged in a very detailed analysis of the pivotal role of birth in population formation. It may appear that we have slighted the role of death. Close reading of the material, however, should cement in the mind the ever presence of death in the form of "Inertial" material.

The fact is that a signal of death, the end of life as it is understood generally, is one of the members of the Gang of 2 in the creation of the individual life. It is an opposite partner of the year of birth. The synthesis of year of birth and age during the Current year is the Current Year, the Year of an Individual Life. Year of birth is the start of life of the individual; age during the Current Year is the end of life to date of that individual.

In the real world this means that every surviving individual (all those, for example, whom the census taker counts), possesses the two ID marks, T(t,r), of which we discussed over and over again in this work. A very significant fact must be understood. When we aggregate the individual lives to form the group of births which will become the Effective Population, these Births separate into their Gang of 2 membership—Survivors and Deaths. The aggregate of the Quantum Cocoons of individual births emerge as Effective Population.

The Velocity of Aggregate Births is made up of the Velocity of Survival and the Velocity of Death. Death is to be interpreted, in our view, as the social counterpart of aging. Age is an attribute of the individual survivor; death, on the other hand, is the corresponding aggregate of individual ages for a group of individuals.

These facts lead to the conclusion that for the individual death inevitably comes after birth. On a social level, therefore, death has the attribute of two distinct states—birth and Inert.

One initial condition facing the start of a new cycle of population formation is the existence of Inertial Births. These represent the social state of births in the state of death. During the Current Cycle they will undergo reproduction, but reproduction that will transform them into Inertial Births with a possible increment. The social aggregate of individuals who make up the Inertial Births is in a death state, and therefore its elements are without conscious wills to create births. They must be first born and then die in order to achieve their reproduction.

The Active Population must be the agents for creating the necessary births. We surmise that the birth state of the Inertial Births occurs as an integral part of the act of Accumulation of Inertial Labor.

On its way as agent of External Labor, the bond that grips the Active Population to the Inertial Births in the Effective Population, must be broken. The energy expended is the energy that creates the birth states of the individuals who make up the Inertial Births.

The death state is accomplished when the consumer goods, on the way as agents of Internal Labor, smashes into the Inertial Births, destroying their birth states while shattering them into dead individual units.

These activities demonstrate the fact that some population members must first born and then die during the Current Cycle. These members are in sync with their life cycle, circumscribed by the length of the cycle of 100 years.

Quantitative stability is the name of the game here insofar as the Inertial Births are concerned.

The other initial condition at the start of the Current Cycle is the initial Active Population. They must be reproduced as Active Population. During the Current Cycle they experience death by being used up in the External Labor System to create the non-human matter which is necessary for the reproduction of the human population. They are reproduced in their active state when the non-human consumer goods are used up in the Internal Labor System.

In this case, the members of the Active Population first die in the External Labor System, and are then born in the Internal Labor System. They die first and then born.

Death, in this case, is the harbinger of the future. It creates the future size of the Inertial Births as well as the future size of the Active Population.

What we are witnessing is the essential and dynamic role of death in all this. In its death state Inertial Births holds a fast grip on the Active Population to maintain the integrity of the Effective Population. In its individual age state it is an indelible component of the birth in the Quantum Cocoon. In both cases, it seems to be in love with the living state of its active companion in its respective Gang of 2.

This leads us to conclude that death is a receptacle, a sink, into which the active energy of the individual or of the population is encapsulated.

It is an essential part of every living individual or of a functioning population. It appears, curiously, like what the physical scientist calls "mass".

Life, then, in a general sense, is a synthesis of birth and age in the case of the individual population member. Births are a synthesis of survivors and deaths in the case of a population.

It follows that death comes to the individual Inertial Birth members when the social process of Internal Labor is in swing. At the same time, death comes to individual Active Population members when the social process of reproduction of non-human goods are in swing.

The upshot of all this is quite fantastic. The death of individual members of the Inertial Births are scattered particles of that battered birth state group. This event takes place as a part of the Accumulation of Inertial Births.

The death of individual members of the Active Population are completely worn out particles of that group. This takes place as part of the reproduction of the non-human matter.

The practical lesson to be drawn from this discourse is that death is an essential element in population formation. On a grand scale it is the inevitable end to the birth of every individual. It manifests itself as the age of the individual, moving ever upward in size and coming to completion sometime between birth and 100 years. During that term of active existence of the individual, it serves as a physical container into which the active energy of the individual is held plantwise bound.

In the dynamical motions of the period of existence, death may be of Inertial Births, a social entity, manifesting itself as chips off the block, as a consequence of population reproduction. Or, it may also be completely exhausted parts of Active Population as a consequence of the creation of the non-human matter.

Death, on a social level, is an inevitable member of the specific Gang of 2, which is Birth. Death, on an individual scale is an inevitable member of the specific Gang of 2, which is Life.

16

Hopes and Speculations

THIS STUDY HAS come to the end of its first phase. It is our hope that it lays the basis for future population studies by up and coming young scholars.

The method employed relied to a large extent on our concept of the Gang of 2 principle of motion. It says that motion is a simple synthesis of opposites; two elements of opposite characteristics join together to form a synthesis which is distinct from either of the two elements.

Motion becomes a dynamic tension between the two opposing partners, resulting in the conversion of one into the other, and conversely. And the aggregation of the synthesis creates a new and different, but related, synthesis. Repetition of this event, with the synthesis married to a specific location in a time-frame, yields a changing activity with respect to time.

We came to this approach after years of pursuing the received ways of studying problems in population formation. Traditional approaches generally concentrate on individual behavior. After all, individuals are the owners of conscious wills which enable them to act autonomously. Hence, defining an appropriate average individual, aggregating (grouping) this average by simple multiplication, is the way to go.

Problem with this approach is that the aggregate result of actions by large numbers of individuals is necessarily dependent on every one of the individuals concerned. However, the specific contribution of any one individual can be equated to zero. This should be widely known by scholars. After all, they subscribe to a principle known as the Central Limit Theorem. This theorem plays a vital role in the formulation of statistical studies. So it is strange that it has not been a corner-stone in the organization of population studies.

The Horse and the Plow

We like to believe that the analysis of the activities of a plow horse would start with a detailed study of land and the plow, their basic characteristics, their history of working together under a variety of circumstances, the obstacles which they must overcome in the performance of their assigned task. The horse's position is always in front; the plow is in the rear of the horse, being pulled forward against the resistance of the earth.

Similarly, the study of any phenomenon requires that we start with a knowledge of what it is we are studying before we explain why it is what is. The mathematician is our model. He or she gives an object a name, say x. Then x is defined in a unique way, distinguishing it from everything else within the theorem that is being created. Whenever x is used in the discourse it cannot have some other identity.

A serious problem, especially in the social sciences, is to postulate the existence of an object which is vaguely described. It is usually given the name of a real object. Then a series of real world policy issues are discussed and resolved about the behavior of this object. An unknown object suddenly takes on a productive life that brings to end some of the great maladies of the world

A case in point is population studies. Almost two centuries ago a published essay made a postulate about population behavior. It did not give us a unique description of what a population is. It went on to discuss serious issues of population policy that had consequences for some of the great laws of the land and for the proper behavior of individuals. Unfortunately, we have determined that much of modern population studies still rely heavily on these ancient and faulty methods.

I propose that we take a tip from the young men and young women who launched the personal computer age. Among other things, they gave us a set of email names. No two individuals, among billions throughout the world, share the same email name.

It is our hope that we will always put the horse before the plow in our analyses.

More on Horse and Plow

In a study of plowing the soil by making central use of a horse, we suggest that we place greatest emphasis on unearthing the attributes of the soil. We cannot start from the assumption that it is not necessary to know anything about the soil; that we must be versed in the capabilities of the horse.

This type of approach should be familiar to the reader. The canonical statistical study begins with an "unknown" universe about which we seek its description. A sample is taken from this universe; some interesting statistics are defined from the sample data; from established statistical theorems these statistics are directly related to parameters of the unknown universe. We then perform tests of significance of the statistics as substitutes for the related, but unknown, parameters of the universe.

If the significance is "great" we accept the conclusion that the specific distribution, of which is defined by the significant parameters is the same as the "unknown" universe. We have come from no knowledge to significant knowledge about an unknown universe.

What's wrong with this picture is it seems too good to be true. We have used a highly developed tool, generally mathematically constructed, to make our analysis. We then use the same set of sample data developed by the use of this tool to make a decision about significance.

We still have no direct knowledge about the unknown universe. We did not study it. We applied a sophisticated tool to analyze some spurious data from that universe.

We statistical scholars have done a magnificent job of creating a tool. We use the tool's best attributes. We confirm that the tool can be used effectively if we have good empirical knowledge about the real universe under study.

This is tantamount to studying the horse at length (as solidified in the statistical theorems). We know much about his attributes, so that the knowledge acquired is about the horse, not the plowing of the land.

Common Sense is Usually Wrong

There exists throughout the knowledge complex a reliance on "common sense". Concepts are created out of some mysterious ability of humans to know the truth. And these truths are enunciated in the face of contradictions by real facts.

The nature of human death is a case in point. Individuals die and go off to heaven or hell. To those who remain alive, the dead subtracts from the living; the more die, the less live. Common sense arithmetic seems to confirm this view.

We have concluded that age is an individual's trait; death is the comparable social attribute. Year of birth is an individual's trait; survival is the comparable social condition. Individual death is manifested by the Velocity of death; aggregate Velocity of Death is the social entity called Inertial Births. Individual year of birth is manifested by the Velocity of Survival; aggregate of Velocity of Survival is the social entity called Active Population.

The two events are not competing. Indeed, they are opposite companions in a Gang of 2, the synthesis of survivors and deaths. They are locked in a process of being converted, one into the other, and conversely. The form of their synthesis is aggregate births, a population level.

These movements of survivors and deaths are what we call reproductive motions. During a given cycle, survivors die and then are reproduced alive. Meantime, dead population members are born and then are reproduced dead. Each is reproduced in its original genre, at the same original quantitative level, with the possibility of adding an increment.

Common sense does not simulate reality.

Miscellanea

We end this work with what we believe to be quite an interesting speculation.

We have shown that the history of annual changes in population formation are made visible from the vantage point of the Current Year. This is so because every specific year of birth plus its age during the Current Year is identically equal to the Current Year. This means that the Velocity of Birth is identical for every specific Quantum Cocoon.

It would seem that this may be a universal principle.

In November 2011 the Hubble telescope observed Galaxy MACS0647-JD, 13.3 billion light years at the edge of the cosmos. We now view this event is a Gang of 2; the earth and that galaxy are opposing partners in a bridge that connects the earth to that distant galaxy. This synthesis is nothing but the present. Now, today, the present time, is the synthesis of the earth and that far away galaxy.

Every annual unit of light along that span of 13.3 billion light years has a velocity of one unit of light per year. This number is 186,000 miles per second.

Here we have an extremely small planet hanging out in a dark and lonely place in the cosmos. On the other extreme is a grandiose galaxy sitting at the outer edge of the cosmos, at a formidable distance from the earth. Yet at this very moment the two are locked in a dance of the universe, from earth to there and from there back to earth, over 13.3 billion light years apart. And it is all taking place at this very moment in time.

It is truly mind-boggling.

This gives us hope that universal principles underlay the behavior of all phenomena.

As we contemplate the future, we picture a panorama of Jewish synagogues, Muslim temples, Christian Churches, and all the gathering places of worship of all the religions of the world. Each worshipper in these holy places proclaims that her/his god is the supreme creator of the universe and of all the laws governing its origin, development, and final outcome. How can this be, when they all seem to disagree on important characteristics of their gods.

Not to worry. There was a secret Unity Conclave among the gods in which they all agreed to the process by which the cosmos was created. It was a joint venture in which the creation was made in concert, the rules governing its function and development and final outcome were set in motion by all. These laws were to be of the reproductive kind, the Gang of 2 variety.

These powerful gods' love of the earth as their prideful creation and of its beloved human denizens led them to make these laws applicable to the earth. They made the earth to be a living, active, planet in the outskirts of the universe. And the reproduction of humans was to be a small-scale reproduction of a piece of earth matter in exactly the same way as the reproduction of the earth itself.

The gods agreed to let their lovable humans go forth and discover the laws of creation of the universe and all that is in it. Let them learn to apply those laws for the benefit of themselves and their posterity. And most of all let their ever-expanding knowledge of these divine principles make them cognizant of the fact that they are themselves pieces of the earth. Out of the earth they were created and into the earth they will return in an ever-recurring magnificent series of reproductive motions.

The earth is human. Humans are the earth. Keep the earth safe and healthy and amenable to develop and grow and make human life peaceable and good.

ABOUT THE AUTHOR

Lloyd Hogan received a master's degree in Economics from the University of Chicago. He has taught economics and statistics at a number of historical black colleges in Virginia, Alabama, Louisiana, Mississippi, North Carolina and Texas. He has been a visiting faculty member at Harvard, Amherst, Cornell, and Gettysburg. He is Emeritus Associate Professor of Economics and Black Studies at Hampshire College, Amherst, MA. He served as editor of the Review of Black Political Economy, Vols. 8-12, 1974-1982. He is the author *of Principles of Black Political Economy*, Routledge and Kegan Paul (Boston, London, 1984)

24002696R00104

Made in the USA
Columbia, SC
17 August 2018